Archibald R. Gibbs

British Honduras

an historical and descriptive account of the colony from its settlement, 1670 -

compiled from original and authentic sources

Archibald R. Gibbs

British Honduras
an historical and descriptive account of the colony from its settlement, 1670 - compiled from original and authentic sources

ISBN/EAN: 9783337312961

Printed in Europe, USA, Canada, Australia, Japan

Cover: Foto ©Andreas Hilbeck / pixelio.de

More available books at **www.hansebooks.com**

BRITISH HONDURAS.

LONDON:
PRINTED BY GILBERT AND RIVINGTON, LIMITED,
ST. JOHN'S SQUARE.

BRITISH HONDURAS:

AN HISTORICAL AND DESCRIPTIVE ACCOUNT OF THE COLONY FROM ITS SETTLEMENT, 1670.

BY

ARCHIBALD ROBERTSON GIBBS, Esq.

" Sub umbra floreo."

COMPILED FROM ORIGINAL AND AUTHENTIC SOURCES.

London :

SAMPSON LOW, MARSTON, SEARLE, & RIVINGTON,

CROWN BUILDINGS, 188, FLEET STREET.

1883.

" I regard the history of British Honduras as affording one of the most remarkable instances of British enterprise and energy."

Sir C. METCALF.—Reply to address on leaving Jamaica, on retiring from the Governorship of that island and its dependencies, dated Fernhill, 9th December, 1842.

CONTENTS.

viii   *Contents.*

BRITISH HONDURAS.

CHAPTER I.

INTRODUCTORY.

WHETHER the result be the splendid acquisition of an Indian Empire, or the comparatively insignificant addition of a small group of islands in the South Seas to our possessions, or the reclamation of a tract of tropical forest from a condition of primeval bush, a record of British enterprise can never fail to prove interesting to British readers.

The reproach that the average Briton, while he may be conversant with the countries of continental Europe, is deplorably ignorant of the more remote portions of that empire upon which the sun never sets—their history, characteristics, and situation—has no longer the force of truth it once had. There is an increasing desire and demand for information respecting our colonial possessions and dependencies.

The colony of British Honduras has hitherto drawn little attention to itself. It has pursued the even tenor of its way without giving trouble to the Colonial Office or bringing its internal affairs prominently before the British public; gaining notoriety neither

B

by intestine complications nor frontier collisions with its neighbours, of any consequence. A small colony, but always a solvent one, it has, nevertheless, offered few inducements to the younger scions of powerful families at home to seek its shores in quest of lucrative public appointments. It has not as yet developed gold-mines or discovered diamond-fields, "struck oil," raised loans, or promoted schemes for quotation on the Stock Exchange. It has, therefore, few representative friends or influential patrons at home to push its interests or disseminate information concerning its resources and capabilities.   .

At present the white element in the population is numerically insignificant, although strongly represented in the wealth and intelligence of the colony. The majority of the inhabitants are coloured creoles, Yucatecan Spaniards, Hispano-Indians or mestizos, sambos, and a few pure Africans, also creole by birth.

The generality of Englishmen when the word Honduras is mentioned allow their ideas to revert to Spanish Honduras Bonds, and the railway fiasco perpetrated in that enterprising republic.

But although its geographical boundaries are limited, its situation geographically—with ready access to the markets of the United States; its topographical features and contour; safe anchorages and convenient harbours along its coast-line, and riverain facilities; its agricultural capabilities; its undeveloped mineral resources; its salubrious climate, immunity from pestilence in an epidemic or endemic form, and from the convulsions of nature which, in the forms of hurricane and earthquake, are wont to devastate tropical regions,

point it out as by no means the least important, while
its unique history renders it not the least interesting,
of our colonial appendages.

In the past, a lazy, lucrative, old-fashioned trade in
mahogany and dyewoods—the latter chiefly logwood
—has been carried on under a system of monopoly, to
the special advantage of some three or four business-
firms who, like monopolists everywhere, have paid
more regard to the protection of their own immediate
gains than—as even a selfish but longer-sighted policy
would have dictated—to the general advancement of
the colony commercially and industrially; retarding
internal development, and checking immigration of any
description above that of coolie labour, and dreading
nothing so much as the introduction of extraneous
energy to interfere with what they considered their
prescriptive rights.

So long as the river-banks and the margins of the
creeks and lagoons supplied an unlimited yield of
noble trees, and mahogany-lumbering and logwood-
cutting could be carried on inexpensively and remune-
ratively; while high prices were maintained in the
London market and the labour difficulty had not arisen,
the short-sightedness of the policy of monopoly was
not apparent.

But the day came when the giants of the forest could
no longer be found as they almost overhung the rivers
and creeks, and had merely to be cut down, roughly
trimmed, pitched into the flood of the wet season, and
rafted down to the ports of embarkation at comparatively trifling cost. Emancipation too had come, and
free labour was gradually getting scarcer and rising

in price. In the good old slave times, and even long
after, the emancipated and their descendants never
grumbled. They worked hard, but it was for "old
massa." Their nine or ten months of arduous toil and
harsh exposure, during which they were well fed and
clothed and housed, according to their wants and
ideas, were cheerfully borne while they were kindly
treated; *they* were all unconscious that a few white
men—or Buckras, as they say—were coining money out
of the sweat of their brows and dusky skins, and they
were made perfectly happy by the six-weeks carnival
of dancing and dissipation annually granted them at
Christmas. But when the black labourer began to
find out the value of his labour—when good wood
grew scarce along the waterways, so that "huntsmen"
had to be employed to search for them in the depths
of the forests—when miles of expensive truck-paths
required to be cut to where the trees had been marked
out—and when from various causes, such as a change
of fashion in the matter of furniture, the substitution
of iron ships for wooden ones, prices went down at
home, monopoly received its death-blow.

It became evident, that the colony could no longer
depend entirely upon its original staple exports for
prosperity or even existence. Attention must be
directed to other industries. The rich, virgin soil at
least remained almost untouched.

Experiments were at first made in sugar cultivation.
Some thirty years ago, parties of refugees from Yucatan,
driven into exile by the disturbed state of their own
country, had successfully proved the suitability of the
soil for this branch of agriculture, but their operations

were limited, and went no further in result than the supply of the local markets.

The first to embark in sugar cultivation on a more extended scale and with a view to exportation, either from inexperience or errors in judgment, did not succeed; but it is almost certain that those who have stepped into their places, with the few who have been financially strong enough to persevere, will eventually add this to the other industries of the colony. The wood trade still continues and probably will continue in that category.

There is also at the present time a fair prospect that the cultivation of the cocoa-nut and other tropical fruits, plantains, bananas, oranges, &c., to supply the New Orleans and Philadelphia markets, will prove remunerative. Steamers now call regularly at Belize, engaging in this trade.

The transit trade, once of considerable value, has been adversely affected lately by these very steamers visiting Spanish ports to the southward, but this may be only temporary, and the colony makes up indirectly what it loses this way. There is still a fair trade done in general merchandize with buyers from the interior.

Besides fortnightly mails to New Orleans, there is an unsubsidized line to that port, a line of steamers to Philadelphia, one to New York, and one to London *viâ* Jamaica.

The colony is in a transition state. Its prospects are promising, its financial condition unembarrassed. All that is wanted is additional capital and increased energy to develop its magnificent resources.

It is in view of the colony's taking a fresh start, and being drawn more closely into the comity of nations by the introduction of steam communication, the submarine and terrestrial telegraph, and, we hope, railways by-and-by, that it has been deemed opportune to put forth this slight account of its past history, present condition, and future prospects.

CHAPTER II.

THE map of Central America shows on the Atlantic Discovery.
side a wide triangular bay of the Caribbean Sea whose
base is formed by the northern shore of Spanish Honduras, one side by the coast-line of British Honduras
and the peninsula of Yucatan, the other by an ima-
ginary line drawn from Cape Catoche to Cape Gracias
á Dios. This bay is studded with numerous islands and
its inner basin protected by a continuous line of coral
reefs. De Solis, the Spanish historian of the Conquest 1502.
of Mexico, claims for the island of Cozumel,[1] a little to
the southward of Cape Catoche, at the northern extremity of the bay, the honour of being the first land
made by Columbus on quitting Cuba and Jamaica on
his continued voyage in search of a passage to the
Pacific. Herrera, another Spanish writer, states that
Bartolomé Columbus arrived at Punta Casinas on the
17th of August, 1502, and landing, took possession of
the country in the name of his most Catholic Majesty
of Spain, calling it Honduras, from the Spanish word
"hondura," depth, the soundings along the coast having

[1] Isle of Swallows.

been found unusually deep by the Spaniards, especially close in shore. Yet another account makes the island touched by the great Columbus on this occasion Bonaca, one of a group called the Bay Islands, in which are also Ruatan and Utila at the southern extremity of the bay. It is probable that the whole bay was exposed by the expedition of Columbus groping for the desiderated passage to the Indies, but Yucatan was properly first discovered by Dias de Solis y Pinzon in 1509. It was in 1519 that Cortez and his warlike companions landed in Yucatan to commence in Tabasco the conquest of Mexico, the record of which is a series of marvels.

1509.
1519.

Towards the solution of the hitherto insoluble problem of how the western continent originally became peopled and a final answer to the speculations of ethnologists upon the origin of the mystic races found inhabiting it, that portion of it which unites the two grand divisions of it, Central America with the southern portion of Mexico, has furnished the greatest accumulation of data. The explorer penetrating the forest-wilds of that region comes suddenly upon remains of what were once magnificent temples and palaces, the ruins and semi-obliterated circumvallations of extensive cities, hieroglyph-covered obelisks and sculptured columns half buried by the dense overgrowth of the jungle. At Chalhuacan or Palenque, at Tulha or Quirigua, among the coffee of Copan, at Utatlan and Patanamit, in the Central States, are discovered the ruined remains of cities covering spaces equal in extent to the area of Rome or Paris.

Aborigines.

Although the Indian tribes inhabiting Mexico and

Central America are not to be confounded with the "haughty red men of the north," made familiar to our youth in the romances of Marryat and Fenimore Cooper, or the cannibal savages of Patagonia, they would appear to evidence an affinity of race and language with them—the type modified by a tropical climate and other causes. Into the theories of an oriental origin or into any of the various speculations of an Israelitish, Egyptian, or Phœnician derivation, it is beyond the scope of this work to enter, but the prominent cheek-bones, copper-coloured complexion, high contracted forehead, long, black, straight hair, small hands and feet, point to a community of origin between the tribes inhabiting Central America and the men of the tomahawk and calumet. In stature they are lower, but as active and muscular, more fleshy, yet less disinclined to physical labour. They are more docile, less given to the pursuits of war and the chase, more sensual.

The aboriginal Indian tribes met by the Spaniards on their advance into Central America would seem to have been branches of a great nation inhabiting the southern portion of Mexico—the Toltecs. Juarros, in his "History of Guatemala," writes the name Tualtec. At the conquest this nation must have been divided into many tribes, the chief of which were the Quiché, Kachiquel, and Zutugil. Yucatan was—still is—peopled to a great extent by the Mayas, the Mosquito Shore by Waikas or Waiknas, remnants of which tribe still exist, and stray specimens may be seen in Belize daily. Other tribal names have come down to us in the existing names of certain localities, such as Poyais, Jicaque, Chiapas, &c.

According to Fuentes, the Toltec king or chief Nimaquiché (great chief), the fifth who reigned in Tula, was directed by an oracle to migrate with his people from Mexico to the south. Like the wanderings of the Israelites, from whom they claim descent,[2] in the desert, the migration of the Toltecs occupied many years. It is stated by the historian above-quoted that Nimaquiché and his people found the region upon which they entered already inhabited. Acxopil, the successor of Nimaquiché, divided the newly-acquired western Canaan between himself and his two sons. Quiché he retained, Kachiquel he gave to his eldest son Jiutemal, who has given its name, it is supposed, to Guatemala, and the third kingdom, Zutugil, to Axiqual, his youngest.

The names of seventeen kings of this dynasty have reached posterity, the last of whom was Sequechul. During the reign of the fourteenth, Kicah-Tanub, the threatened invasion by the Spaniards of Mexico took place.

Prior to the invasion the country was the scene of sanguinary internecine conflict. Axiqual first invaded the territory of his brother Jiutemal, and from that date war raged for many generations. Again, after an interval of peace, in the reign of Balam-Acan, the

---

[2] Fuentes relates that he obtained from Father Francisco Vasquez, the historian of the Order of St. Francis, a MS. of Don Juan Torres, grandson of the last king of the Quichés, a document in which the Toltecs claim to be Israelites, who, after crossing the Red Sea, fell into idolatry, and from fear of Moses fled westwards under a chief Tanub, and passing from one continent to the other (? how) reached Mexico.

king of the Zutugils Zutuguilepob abducted from the royal palace of Utatlan, Ixconsocil, the daughter of Balam-Acan of Quiché, his friend. This Mexican edition of the rape of Helen led to sanguinary wars, which lasted, with few short intervals, down to the arrival of Alvarado on his conquering march southwards. The warlike weapons of the contending nations consisted chiefly of missiles—stones hurled by slings, poisoned arrows and javelins, pikes and swords, or pieces of wood (macanos) into which roughly sharpened stones (chay) were set like teeth, which did great execution. They were also provided with shields made of the skin of the "danta." [3] The forces on either side varied (according to Juarros) from 60,000 to 120,000, and the slaughter during their engagements was frequently immense.

The capital city of Quiché, Utatlan, was undoubtedly the most opulent found by the Spaniards in this quarter. As it furnished 72,000 combatants against them, it must have been extremely populous. The next in importance was Xelahuh, now Quezaltenango. As it had ten captains over it, and each captain, according to the system of deputed government, ruled over his "Xiquipil," or 8000 dwellings, it therefore contained 80,000 houses, which Fuentes estimates would give 300,000 as its population. Patanamit, or "the city," is in the kingdom of Kachiquel, and was also called Tecpan-Guatemala, which, Vasquez says, means "Royal House of Guatemala," wherefore he infers it was the capital. Among the curious scattered remains of Central America are the circus of Copan, the great stone hammock, and the cave of Tibulca.

[3] Tapir.

Francisco de Fuentes, the chronicler of Guatemala, says the circus of Copan was entire in his time (1702). It is, or was, a circular space enclosed by stone pyramidal columns, eighteen feet high, with figures, male and female, in excellent sculpture, generally in bas-relief, and enamelled. In the centre was the altar. Isolated monolithic remains, profusely ornamented and covered with hieroglyphs, are continually met with in these districts of Guatemala, at Uxmal in Yucatan, and many places in Mexico, all agreeing in archæological character.

Modern interest has been little centred upon these extraordinary relics of the past, and the difficulties in the way of exploration and examination are great. In 1807 a Captain Dupaix explored a portion of them, but the result of his labours was not given to the world until 1834.[4] He had been preceded by Del Rio, and was followed by an American archæologist, named Stephens, who had been previously engaged on Egyptian antiquities. In the opinion of Mr. Stephens, whose operations were curtailed by the war of supremacy then being waged by the Liberals under Morazan and the clerical or reactionist party under Carrera, there is no identity between the sculptured columns and hieroglyphics of the Indian ruins of Central America and those of any eastern nation of antiquity—their present remarkable state of preservation, when the nature of the climate they survive in is considered, not admitting of any great age being assigned to them. The original buildings and monuments were constructed, he thinks, " by the races who

[4] Paris, 1834.

occupied the country at the time of the invasion by the Spaniards, or of some not very distant progenitors."[*]

These races are yet in existence in those countries, many of their numbers still beyond the pale of civilization, living as their ancestors lived under Balam-Acan.

How these people acquired a knowledge of architecture, skill in sculpture, and design in delineation—how buildings of lime and stone, courts, obelisks and idols, ornamented by sculpture and enamel, came to be constructed by them, if the theory of an eastern origin and an antique date are untenable with regard to them, must ever remain one of time's mysteries. Enough, perhaps, that here lie mouldering the remains of a once cultivated, polished, and peculiar people, who passed through the usual vicissitudes incident to nations—rise, progress, and fall.

The descriptions of the Alcazar or king's palace by the Spanish historians recall the pictures of the Alhambra found in the pages of later writers.

The system of government was a pure monarchy, the king ruling, assisted by a council of twenty-four Caciques, or princes of the blood, who had great privileges granted them, and were entrusted with the control of the revenue and administration of justice. In the ten principal cities satraps or lieutenants were appointed to govern as many districts or Xiquipils. They had full power except over the lives and properties of the "ahaun," or heads of noble families.

[*] Explorations are now—1882—being extensively carried on with great success by M. Charnay, under the auspices of Mr. P. Lorillard and other wealthy amateurs.

These satraps also were assisted by councils of the nobles in their government. All public offices were bestowed on persons belonging to the noble class. Marriage of a noble with a plebeian degraded him to the rank of his wife, and carried with it the sequestration of his estate. Their religion was a form of idolatry disgraced by human sacrifices, and the latter circumstance has been adduced as a justification of the cruelty exercised upon them by the Spaniards of the conquest. The worship of the sun, or some form of fire-worship, would appear to have constituted a part of their religious system.

The criminal code contained the punishment of death too frequently for modern ideas, but otherwise seems to have been founded on just principles. Incendiaries were considered enemies of the State on the ground that he who sets fire to a single house may burn down a whole town. Death of the culprit and banishment of his whole family was therefore the sentence in cases of arson. The ordeal of torture disgraced the proceedings in most trials.

Domestic slavery was one of their institutions, and a "simarron" (? origin of Maroon), or runaway, was punished by death on the second offence. For the first he was fined.

According to Torquemada they possessed a superior system of education for the young of both sexes.

Conquest and subjugation. Cortez deputed the conduct of the expedition to Don Pedro de Alvarado, who marched with a numerically insignificant force of Spaniards and about 4000 Mexican allies. It is stated by Juarros that the kings of Mexico and Quiché acknowledged ties of relationship, and that Montezuma, himself, a prisoner, contrived to convey a private message to Kicah-Tanub, to warn him of the intended invasion.

In the course of one year Alvarado, by extra- 1524. ordinary exertions and a series of unparalleled successes, completed the conquest of the three kingdoms, only the wider and more outlying portions of the country remaining in the possession of the Indians. In reviewing the extraordinary achievements of the Spaniards in these regions, it is only possible to account for the rapidity of their conquests over overwhelming numbers by considering that the Indians when they first saw the Spanish cavalry had never set eyes on an animal larger than a tapir, and the roar of fire-arms and artillery were novelties calculated to produce in their minds superstitious dread of a superhuman power rather than to convince them of any physical superiority in their opponents. There was no union amongst the separate Indian kingdoms against the invaders, and failing in his efforts to bring a defensive unity about, and in dread of the Teules (or gods), as the Spaniards were designated, about whom he had received oracular information, Kicah-Tanub died prematurely. Alvarado first entered the district of Soconuzco, inhabited by the tribe of the Pipiles, 1524 but quickly turned his attention to Xelahuh, or Quezaltenango, the largest fortified place in Quiché, to which he fought his way against the numerous forces collected by Tecum-Unam, the son and successor of Kicah-Tanub. The final struggle took place on the plains of Itzacapa, when Alvarado, with his cavaliers and their allies, defeated an army of 250,000.[6] Alvarado slew Tecum himself with a lance-thrust.

Chinanivalut, his son, now began to treat with the invaders, and invited Alvarado and his followers to visit him at the capital, Utatitlan. The Spaniards complied, and entered the royal city, but their suspicion of treachery being aroused, they withdrew from it, and encamped on the plains close to the city. Here Alvarado was visited by the king of Quiché. Alvarado having found that treachery was intended, tried Chinanivalut, and hanged him on the spot. The Indians now attacked the Spaniards with desperate fury, but were met with equal bravery, and routed, abandoning a field covered with their dead and wounded. The capital and kingdom of Quiché were in the hands of the bold invaders. Alvarado had the wisdom to continue the semblance of native royalty in Quiché, while he turned his attention to the subjugation of Kachiquel (Guatemala) and Zutugil. Sinacan, king of Guatemala, had already sent him ambassadors with presents of gold while he was at Utatitlan.

Leaving Leon Cardona to command in Quiché, the chief invader entered the capital of Sinacan, his new ally, who persuaded him to direct his arms against Zutugil, the third division of the empire of Quiché, the capital of which was on the Lake Atitlan, a rocky fastness in the highlands. One engagement subdued the Zutugils, who became the allies of the Spaniards, even remaining faithful during the subsequent revolt of the Quiché and Kachiquel Indians from Spanish domination. Sinacan had meanwhile voluntarily submitted.

[6] Juarros.

Thus was the empire of Quiché in its three divi-   1525.
sions subdued—Quiché proper, Kachiquel, and Zutugil.
Revolts, it is true, had subsequently to be quelled;
but 1530 may be quoted as the year of the consolidation of the Spanish conquests in Central America,
and the foundation of the kingdom or captain-generalship of Guatemala.

The city was founded in 1527. It was destroyed   1527.
by the falling of a body of water from the crater
of an extinct volcano, and rebuilt in 1541 on the ·
spot now occupied by " La Antigua." Constant
destruction by, and alarms of, earthquake led to its
removal in 1773 to the valley of Las Vacas, where it
now stands. Salvador and Nicaragua (caciqueships)
were taken possession of by Pedrarias Davilla about
the same period.

Cortez, meanwhile, had taken separate measures for
the subjugation of the country on the Atlantic side.
Christoval de Olid had landed in Guimara (Honduras)
and founded cities there. De Olid would appear to
have set up for himself, or, at least, to have acted
independently of Cortez and Alvarado, and Las Casas
was despatched by Cortez to subdue him. De Olid,
at first victorious, was betrayed and murdered by his
companions. Las Casas thus obtained quiet possession
of the city of Trujillo. Cortez himself performed one
of the most remarkable journeys ever made with a
military force, from Mexico by way of Itza or Peten to
Honduras. While there, he founded a sea-port town
and called it Puerto Caballos—now Puerto Cortez in
the Republic of Honduras.

Subsequent to the discovery of this peninsula   Yucatan,
1508-16.

by De Solis, an expedition left Cuba during the captain-generalship of Diego Velasquez, under Francisco Hernandez de Cordova, a rich planter of the island. In reality it was composed of a band of adventurers fired by the spirit of the epoch— "de buscar nuevas tierras."[7] They hit off Cape Catoche or Cotoch, which received the name from the incident of the Indians who came off, bringing food and water in their canoes to De Cordova's ships, crying in their language "conex cotoch!" So the guttural Maya sounded to the Latin-tongued Spaniards, but the cry was, "conex notoch" (conesh notosh as it is pronounced, or in old Maya, conex kotoch), meaning "come home"—an invitation to the Spaniards to land. Campeché (Kimpech) and Pontachan, Indian towns, were visited, and Bernal Diaz describes the "adoratorios," or temples containing idols. During the hostilities which subsequently took place, the general, De Cordova, received ten wounds from poisoned arrows, of which he died at Cuba on his return; the adventure cost the Spaniards, besides their general, seventy-two soldiers. Two Indians, christened by the chaplain of the expedition, Alonso Gonzalez, respectively Julian and Melchor, were taken to Cuba. Some gold in the dust brought with them, excited the cupidity of the Spaniards at the Havana and Velasquez equipped a second expedition, which he entrusted to Juan de Grijalva. Pedro de Alvarado, the future conqueror of the empire of Quiché, Alonzo Dávila, and Francisco de Montejo, all hidalgos of Spain, accompanied Grijalva. Leaving the port of

1517.

[7] B. Diaz Herrera.

Matanzas on the north side of Cuba and doubling Cape Antonio, they sighted the island of Cozumel (Cuzumil —isla de golandrinas). On landing, the soldiers were surprised to hear the language of Jamaica, with which they were partially acquainted.[8] Inquiry produced the information that, two years. before, ten Indians had crossed in a canoe from Jamaica to Cozumel; a voyage which in a slight measure may account for the dispersion of Indian tribes over these latitudes. Grijalva pushed on to Pontachan, in Campeché, taking the Jamaicans with him. Tabasco was taken possession of in the name of the Spanish king.[9] Soon after this, Benito Martinez was made Bishop of Yucatan, the first bishop of New Spain. In 1519 Hernando Cortez arrived in Cozumel, and the subjugation of Tabasco and Yucatan was completed by him, and Montejo under him, before Cortez left Mexico on his famous journey to Honduras. The city of Vera Cruz had also been founded.

1519.

1521.

Yucatan previous to its occupation and subsequent pacification, in the time of Cortez and Montejo, had no common name, but was divided into districts under chiefs, as that of Cepech, of Choaca, of Chacan; unless the name of the principal city, Mayapan, was applied to the whole peninsula. Various origins are given to the name Yucatan. Some make it a corruption of Tectetan, a town in the interior : others derive it from "yucca," a root (Adam's needle) from which cakes are made, the Indian substitute for bread, some from the expression "Yucatta a tan," used by the natives to the first discoverers, and meaning "we do not understand you."

[8] Diaz Herrera.   [9] Fra. Cogolludo.

Soon after the conquest, Spanish missionaries entered upon the more worthy subjugation of the country by the conversion of the Indians to Christianity, visiting the wildest parts, and displaying their wonted zeal. Especially zealous was an amiable Dominican named Bartolomé las Casas. But even to the present day, in the wilds of the mountains of Central America roam numbers of "Lascandones," or unbaptized Indians, probably following the idolatrous traditions of their Toltec ancestors.

CHAPTER III.

A HALO of romance surrounds the early history of British Honduras, legend assigning this region as the scene of many a daring exploit, many a riotous orgie, in the good old times when the adventurous sons of Albion roamed the Caribbean, partly under the pro-tection of their own dreaded black flag, and sometimes under that of the country of their birth, which did not wholly cast them off while their depredations were confined to his Catholic Majesty's galleons and settle-ments on the Main.

The central hero of this romance was a Scottish rover named Wallace, or Wallis, "who so distinguished himself," naively remarks the Honduras Almanac fifty-six years ago, "by acts of bravery and desperation that his name became a terror to the Spaniards." His name is supposed to survive in that of the town of Belize, which is considered a Spanish corruption of Wallis. In the Spanish language there is no W, and Wallis became Vallis, and as V is sounded by Spaniards almost as B, the transition to Ballis, Balize, and finally Belize, is easily understood. The Indian name of Belize is Mopan; of Honduras, Zuina.

It is sufficiently a matter of history that the seas in this part of the world were so far back as the time of our own Charles I. infested by hordes of pirates of our own and other nations, the homeward-bound, richly-laden merchant-ships of Spain offering the inducement to the more adventurous spirits of our rising navy to embark in such questionable enterprises. Letters of marque were issued, but gentlemen of the stamp of Mr. Wallace, or Wallis, were not wont to be very particular about the nature of their ships' papers in days when they were not likely to be frequently overhauled by our ubiquitous cruisers, and were probably satisfied with the roving commission and immunity from search given them by our national hostility to Spain at that era.

The Bay of Honduras, with its numerous islands and shore inlets, and its protecting reefs—the navigation of which was ticklish work for the clumsy vessels of war of the period, but which they were familiar with—its creeks, lagoons, and river-mouths densely shrouded by tropical foliage, was doubtless early selected by the bold buccaneers as safe retreating-ground whence to retire with the spoils of, and enjoy a respite from, their successful sea-forays.

But these gallant Turpins of the rolling main were not the class of men to found a peaceful and thriving settlement. It is on record that most of them, becoming regular pirates, and no longer confining their attention to Spanish vessels, but considering all to be fish that came into their net, met an exalted fate at Kingston, Jamaica; while the persistent efforts of our cruisers, as well as those of other nations, eventually

dispersed them, and buccaneering became an un-
profitable avocation.

The portion of the province of Yucatan now known
as British Honduras (British Yucatan it has been
called) would never appear to have been occupied by
the Spaniards, but left in possession of the Indian
tribes of Chols and Mopan.

The original settlement by the British of this part
of the Spanish Main cannot be authentically traced to
any date farther back than the Protectorate of Cromwell, when it was used by them as a place of retreat
from Spanish men-of-war in the desultory warfare
carried on by us and that nation in these distant
localities, at times without regard to the terms upon
which the Courts of Madrid and St. James's happened
to be with each other.

In 1638 a few British sailors were wrecked on
the coast of Yucatan and would appear to have
settled.

In 1655 the island of Jamaica was taken from the
Spaniards by Penn, one of Cromwell's admirals,
assisted by Venables. Indeed it was about this
period, under the vigorous foreign policy of the
Protector, England first seriously turned her attention
to conquest and colonization in this part of the world.
It was about this time also that the value of the woods
growing in tropical America first began to attract
attention, and to be sought after as articles of trade
and commerce. If, as by the adoption of her " totem "
and appropriate motto, the colony of British Honduras
would appear to consider herself indebted (at all events
for past prosperity) mostly to another tree, it is to

1638.

1655.

logwood she certainly owes in the first instance her existence.

It was at one time the practice of the class of privateers (almost identical with buccaneers) cruising against Spanish traders to set fire to all vessels they captured which might be laden with logwood, having first stripped them of everything valuable.

But it so happened that a Captain James, the master of a letter of marque, having captured a Spanish vessel [1] the cargo of which consisted of this wood, brought the ship and cargo into the Port of London. On endeavouring to dispose of the latter he was gratified as well as surprised to find for it a ready sale at an enormous price per ton. The crew, who had used up a portion of the precious freight to burn in the galley-fire, had little idea that they were using fuel at a *hundred pounds* per ton during the voyage!

The fame of this dyewood soon spread, and privateers were fitted out and despatched to cruise off the Main, for the especial capture of logwood-laden vessels, on their passage home to Spain from his Catholic Majesty's possessions in the "Indies."

In course of time, as prizes became scarcer, protecting cruisers of the Spanish navy more abundant, the crews of the privateers found it more profitable to search for the wood on shore, cut it, and load 1667. their vessels with it. Earl Sandwich's Treaty of Madrid finally compelled the abandonment of privateering in these waters, and the crews naturally enough turned their cutlasses into machétes, and commenced to lop his Spanish Majesty's forest-trees on shore when they no longer were permitted to cut off

[1] Honduras Almanacs, 1826-27.

with impunity his lieges' heads and limbs on the high seas.

Ruatan or Roatan, sometimes called Rattan, one of the group known as the "Bay Islands," long after- wards a bone of contention between England and Spain, was first captured by the English in 1642. The group lies just off Trujillo, a canoe-trip from the mainland. **1642.**

The Spanish colonial authorities did not submit tacitly to this British occupation of the Bay Islands. The pious zeal of the Bishop of Comayagua, metropoli- tan of Guatemala, was first roused, and in turn stimu- lated the warlike energy of the Governors of Cuba and Guatemala, and of the President of the Audencia of San Domingo, who equipped a joint expedition to expel the heretics.

Four ships of war, under the command of General Francisco de Villalba y Toledo, arrived in the harbour of Ruatan, and commenced the attack. **1650.**

The attempt to dislodge the British was unsuccessful, and Villalba re-embarked and sailed for Santo Tomas de Castilla.[2] The Spaniards under Villalba were foiled by the resolute defence and the natural strength of the place.

On the 4th of March, 1650, the Governor of Guate- mala, Antonio de Lara Mongrobejo, despatched rein- forcements, ammunition, and supplies, collected from Guatemala and Chiquimula, to Villalba, who thereupon proceeded to renew the attack. Profiting by his pre- vious experience, the Spanish general made the second attempt from a different point. Determined resistance was again offered by the British defenders; but having effected a breach in their entrenchments, the Spaniards stormed and carried the place.

[2] Juarros.

In their subsequent march upon the town the attacking force suffered greatly from the heat by day, miasma by night, and venomous reptiles and insects at all times. They found the place evacuated, the garrison having removed themselves and their valuables on board their ships, and entirely abandoned the island.[3]

Very shortly after this expulsion of our countrymen from the Bay Islands a few English sailors attacked 1759. and took Campeché. The town had been previously visited by a buccaneer, William Park, in 1640, and pillaged, according to Fr. Diego Lopez de Cogolludo, of the Order of St. Francis, who has written a history of Yucatan. The British corsairs were in fact like a cloud of mosquitoes buzzing around the Spanish possessions in this quarter of the globe.

1662. But the first regular establishment of English logwood-cutters was made in 1662 by adventurers, probably from Jamaica, incited by the increasing demand for logwood. Their numbers were soon augmented by fresh arrivals, and extending southwards from Cape Catoche, they in a short space of time spread as far as the River Belize, and westwards to what appears to have been then called the lake and island of Triste (between Tabasco and the River Campeton), a lagoon with an island in the middle of it. At this time there were two places of rendezvous, or market-places, for the early settlers—the mouth of the Belize River and this island of Triste, adjacent to Campeché.

1667. The operations of these adventurous colonizers were at length the subject of negotiations between the re-

---

[3] Juarros, "History of Guatemala." Translated, London, 1811.

spective Governments of England and Spain, and in
1667 it is stipulated that in case of war the subjects of
the two countries settled in these regions shall give each
other six months' notice before commencing hostilities.

It is allowable to infer from the mutual animosity
existing between the two nationalities at this time,[4] the
well-known jealousy shown by the Spaniards of other
nations, and especially of the English, encroaching on
the lands they had discovered and occupied, and the
slight regard paid in these remote countries to treaties
made in Europe, that the stipulation above referred to
had little force in the Bay, and that private encounters
quite irrespective of the fact of peace or war existing
between the parent countries, frequently took place
without previous warning. But the resolute Baymen
had got a grip, and with all the bull-dog tenacity of
their race they refused to let go, despite the strenuous
efforts of the Spanish colonists to shake them off.

By article vii. of the Godolphin Treaty of 1670,   1670.
Spain ceded to Great Britain in perpetuity right of
sovereignty over all lands in America and the West
Indies held by her at the time.[5]

It is difficult to reconcile this absolute concession
with subsequent treaties between the high contracting
parties, in which special reference is made to the Hon-

---

[4] "The Udaller added his voice potential: 'There is never
peace with Spaniards beyond the line. I have heard Captain
Tragondacke and honest old Commodore Rummalaer say so a
hundred times, and they have both been down in the Bay of
Honduras, and all thereabouts.' "—"The Pirate," by Sir. W.
Scott.

[5] Bryan Edwards, vol. i. p. 175, "History of West Indies."

duras wood-cutters, granting them only the privileges
of "cutting, loading, and carrying away," but refusing
permission for the establishment of permanent plantations beyond mere provision-grounds, and safe-
guarding, in distinct terms, the sovereign rights of
the King of Spain and the Indies.

But on the promulgation of Sir William Godolphin's
treaty logwood-cutting establishments rapidly increased
in number, and the population of the settlement rose
to 700 whites. As yet no negroes had been introduced. Among the settlers was the notorious Admiral
Benbow and his partner in wood-cutting, a person
named Jenkins. Benbow, re-entering active service
in the navy, left his interests in the hands of his co-
labourer, and, according to the story told, was considerably astonished, on being stationed at Port Royal years
afterwards, at the appearance on board his flag-ship of
Jenkins, desirous of handing him over his share of the
profits *ad interim.* A creek on which the admiral and his
partner Jenkins worked is still known as Benbow Creek.

1671.   Writing in 1671 to the king—Charles II.—Sir
Thomas Lynch, Governor of Jamaica, reports that the
settlement of British Honduras "increased his Majesty's customs and the national commerce more than any
of his Majesty's Colonies "—a statement obviously not
founded on statistical information, but, as the report
was called for by "the Lords in Council," proving in-
disputably that the settlement had thus early attracted
official notice, and must therefore have attained considerable importance.

1675.   Four years afterwards the Spaniards attacked the
British at the lake and island of Triste, capturing

260 of them, and carrying them prisoners to the mines of Mexico.

Campeché was retaken in 1678; but a couple of 1678-80. years subsequent to this recapture the British settlers would appear to have abandoned all attempts to secure a permanent footing on the other side of Cape Catoche.

The settlers on the Hondo, New and Northern Rivers, and the River Belize, enjoyed comparative immunity from attack, the position of these settlements lying out of the track of armed Spanish vessels passing to and fro the Gulf of Mexico, while those in the Bay of Campeché were constantly exposed to onslaughts. The more northern colonists, for this reason, then, retired to the remote and less exposed points beginning to be permanently settled by their compatriots; where they were at liberty to pursue their avocations to greater profit when not compelled so frequently to abandon them in order to repel sudden invasions.

To the same spots the extension of the logwood trade continued to send accessions from neighbouring British colonies in America and the West Indies— chiefly from Jamaica.

At this point there is a hiatus in the chronicles 1680— of the colony. Indeed the records—especially re- 1717. lating to the period prior to 1762—are altogether meagre in interesting or useful data. Most of the documents were lost beyond recovery in the invasion of the settlement by the Spaniards in 1779. Some few were carried to the Havana, and brought back after the return from the captivity which followed that disaster, but were subsequently scattered in the hurricane of 1787. Another loss is supposed to have occurred when the ship *Triumvirate* went down off St. George's Caye; but why public documents were on board of that vessel is not clear.

It may be presumed, however, that the settlers were left in a great measure undisturbed in their operations, and to consolidate their institutions, increase their trade, and swell their population.

1717. In the year 1717 the Board of Trade and Plantations addressed a memorial to his Majesty George I., asserting our right by treaty to cut logwood in those parts. The only treaty, as far as we know, yet in existence giving any such rights, which the memorial could refer to, is that already quoted of 1670. The memorial had no decisive result. It is useful in showing by returns the quantity of logwood imported into England in four successive years.

		Tons	cwt.	qr.	lb.
1713	. . . .	2189	15	3	22
1714	. . . .	4878	14	3	24
1715	. . . .	5863	12	1	14
1716	. . . .	2032	17	2	9
		14,995	0	3	9

but, says the memorial, " the price is at present reduced from 40*l.* to 16*l.* per ton." The falling off in the quantity imported in 1716 is somewhat unaccountable.

1718. Considerable alarm was created in the year 1718 by the fitting out of an expedition by the Spaniards at Peten, an Indian town on a lake of the interior at the head of the Belize River. The whole district of Peten is now the most peaceful and retired portion of the Republic of Guatemala, inhabited by Peteneros or Spaniards of mixed Indian descent.

In defiance of the six months' notice in case of an outbreak of hostilities clause of the treaty of 1667, the Spaniards secretly prepared a strong expeditionary force at this interior town and advanced to the head of the Old River, north-west branch, with the intention of dispossessing the British. They advanced with great caution and erected fortifications at the head of the river. The settlers in that vanward position, however, had received intelligence of the incursion and had made preparations for resistance, and even had time to send for aid to the king of the Mosquito Shore, which that mighty potentate afforded. There is thus traditional record of a good and satisfactory cause for our subsequent friendly relations with that monarchy, and our throwing the ægis of our protection in turn over him and his realm. General Shute, Governor of Massachussets, having heard of the intended attack, dispatched H.M.S. *King George,* Captain William Weir, to the assistance of the Baymen. The Spaniards, however, contented themselves with sending a few look-out craft down the river, and as these never returned, they made no further move. The stronghold they had erected at the head of the river was occupied by an outpost for several years. The site is now known as Spanish Look-out, and remains of the fort were to be traced there some years ago, and possibly are still in existence.

The introduction of negro slaves appears to belong to this period. They were not, however—at first, at all events—brought from Africa but from our neighbouring colonies, which had already imported them to a considerable extent.

CHAPTER IV.

EARLY SETTLEMENT (*continued*).

A BACKWOODS life in British Honduras in those days must have been, for those who entered upon it, an arduous, adventurous and precarious one. Arduous it still continues; but it could only have been by constant and unusual exertions that a small body of white men could' have realized fortunes—even with higher market prices for their products—by penetrating into the heart of the primeval forests, hitherto untrodden, and of which the vegetation was dense beyond conception, and tearing from them the huge logs and ship-loads of valuable billets—and the logs of those days were giants. It is true they had not as yet to clear miles of broad truck-paths into the woods, but the tropical jungle had to be cleared in the immediate neighbourhood of their operations. They had to paddle themselves months' supplies of provisions, utensils, tools, and rough articles of furniture, long distances against strong flowing river currents and rapids, up difficult creeks; they had their bush-huts and storehouses for the season of labour to construct; they had to endure a trying climate, myriads of flies, exposure to wet weather, danger from noxious reptiles, and were liable at any moment to attack from their inveterate enemies the Spaniards. Yet the hardy, resolute Baymen, faced difficulty and danger cheerfully, displayed patient endurance of toil and hardships, and indomitable courage whenever the enemy attempted to drive them away.

The vessels carrying away their wood would certainly bring them provisions and general merchandize, besides which they would seem early to have had intimate relations with our North American colonists. In those early days even, they imported some of the comforts and luxuries of more civilized countries, and have ever shown an appreciation of the elegancies of life, notwithstanding their rough mode of existence. They displayed great shrewdness in managing their internal affairs, an acquaintance with the elementary laws of political economy, and prudence and foresight in drawing up simple rules for self-government. They were lovers of freedom always; men whose mental calibre matched their physical stamina.

The following, extracted from an old Guatemala gazette, must of course be accepted "cum grano salis," but it suffices to show how much in early days the settlers required treaty protection. The date is October, 1730.

"News has been received that a privateer from Campeché, with a patent or licence from the governor, arrived along the seas, in a well-armed brigantine, and seized, on the River Belize, seven English brigs and sloops, upon which they went with them to Campeché, and a few days after, being encouraged by the governor, and accompanied by another vessel, they went to Bacalar, whither they took six cannons of large calibre, sent by the governor, which were mounted in the new fortress of San Felipe, and accompanied by the prisoners of the fortress with the Spaniard Don Alonzo Figaroa, by order of the governor, and they did as the Castilian had commanded them ; they penetrated with two brigs thirty-nine miles up the New River, and they travelled across by land from New River, on the transit of which they made prisoners sixteen Englishmen and an Englishwoman with her daughter, sixteen negroes and four negresses. They burnt thirty hamlets or ranchos full of logwood, which the English had got ready to embark, and they burnt in Belize altogether twenty-four vessels ; and having collected a great number of axes, saws, and other tools used for the cutting of wood, they came away without having been attacked by the English, who retreated into the bush to avoid greater damage, and the expedition returned to Campeché on the 20th June, 1730."

This bombastic account of what was an ordinary foray of the time, throws a faint ray of light on the condition of the settlement at this period, and that is perhaps all it is useful for as an extract.

But, despite occasional inroads on its peace and quiet, the colony established itself, and increased in importance and in population.

1738. Prior to the year 1738, the inhabitants chose seven magistrates to administer justice, control finance, and undertake any measures necessary for the public good and safety. These magistrates no doubt held sessions at stated periods—the adumbration of future grand and supreme and summary courts ; but they were severally stationed or appointed to dispense a rough kind of justice at the different points on the rivers and lagoons where logwood and mahogany works had been established—performing the duties of district-magistrates in short, and exercising a kind of family sovereignty, each within his own bounds. This simple and only form of government, concurrent with the preservation of loyal allegiance to the crown, suited the settlers, who long remained attached to their "ancient usages and customs." · But in this year they elected a certain Henry Sharpe, Esq., as their superintendent, who was probably nothing more than the presiding magistrate or chairman of the magisterial body, as the annual election of magistrates was not altered, or their functions or powers curtailed. The same simple patriarchal rule was continued until 1741, when we find that two commissioners, Robert Hodgson and William Pitt, were sent out by the home government. Ruatan and the Mosquito Shore were included in these gentlemen's commission, and during their execution of it, they resided principally at the latter places. They made no alterations in the mode of government, and the elective magistracy was continued without interruption down to the year 1765.

Attack by the British on Trujillo. Ruatan and 1742. Bonaca were occupied by a British force, and a governor appointed in the king's name.

As early as 1740 attempts had been made by English adventurers to settle on the Mosquito Shore, an Indian coast-territory never subdued entirely by the Spaniards, but their efforts not proving successful their acts were disavowed by our government.

Even at this date a project to form a connexion by

canal between the Atlantic and Pacific, across this portion of the American continent, *viâ* the San Juan River and the Lake of Nicaragua, had received at-tention in England : hence the attempts to effect an occupation of the Mosquito Coast.

1744. In this year it was recommended to the king in council that a legislative body should be formed for the purpose of drawing up a constitution for British Honduras founded on the laws of England.

Whether this was the result of an application on the part of the inhabitants of the Bay themselves or not, does not clearly appear, but the presumption, consider-ing their attachment to the simple form of government by elected magistrates, is to the negative view. It may have been brought on by representations from the executive of Jamaica to the home authorities, or, which, is still more probable, have been produced by some report furnished by Messrs. Hodgson and Pitt on com-pletion of their commission in the year 1741. It was, if entertained, not followed by any action.

1754. The Spaniards were aware that an attack upon the settlement from the sea was unlikely to be success-ful. The intricate navigation amongst the islands and shoals of the Bay, better known to the Baymen than to them, was an obstacle to any maritime force. Ex-asperated, however, by the continued prosperity of the British wood-cutters, they again, in the year 1754, determined on a land expedition to drive the persistent intruders from their territory.

Accordingly, a second time a large force was got together at Peten in the year 1754.

The Spaniards mustered to the number of 1500, and

marched upon the Old River Works, and reached
Labouring Creek, a tributary of that river, unopposed.
But here they were met by a couple of hundred cutters
with their slaves, and defeated.

On this, as on other occasions, the slaves proved
their courage—which is no uncommon trait in African
nature—and their fidelity—which perhaps is more
remarkable—to their masters. There is only one way
to account for the invariable fidelity evinced by
the slaves employed in wood-cutting in Honduras.
Instead of the degraded bondage and grinding toil
which was the lot of slaves on plantations, the logwood
and mahogany-cutter was a slave only in name. He
was not driven in a gang to his daily toil, but worked
side by side with his master, sharing with him the
unrestricted life of the backwoods, well fed, performing the noble work of the axeman, which in itself
has a smack of freedom about it, his cutlass, or
machéte, as it is called, always by his side. Slavery
in Honduras brought with it the same social evils it
introduced elsewhere, and the effects of it as an institution are to be discerned still in the laxity of morals
and minor social blemishes characteristic of the
present mixed population, but it presented less harsh
features, and no such atrocities as marked its existence
elsewhere.

The war between England and Spain which com-   1759.
menced in 1759 was closed by the Treaty of Paris in
1763.

The British settlers had now gained a tolerably firm
footing in Central America.

It is difficult on any principle of international law

to justify the conduct of the early settlers in thus persistently thrusting themselves upon territory which another nation had fought and bled for, and which was theirs both by right of original discovery and conquest. It is equally so to exonerate the home government from a share in the blame, for if they were chary of recognizing the settlement during its infancy, or at first in affording aid or protection to the settlers, they unquestionably winked at their doings, and as the intrusive project progressed and developed a permanent character of occupancy, the authorities at home began to take greater interest in the settlement. But it must be borne in mind that during the progress of British Honduras England was almost constantly at war with Spain, and that a system of reprisals was kept up between the two countries in these far-off localities but little governed by treaty stipulations or the relation existing between the two powers in Europe.

The treaty of 1763 extorted from Spain a recognition of the right of his Britannic Majesty's subjects to "cut, load, and carry away" logwood unmolested, to occupy their houses and magazines, but stipulated the demolition of all fortifications and reserved Spanish sovereignty in the soil.

1754.

The Spanish colonial authorities took advantage of these stipulations of this treaty to push their interference with the operations of the wood-cutters to the point of exasperation. "Fortunately," says a writer in the *Honduras Observer*, in 1841, "for the present race, we feel nothing of the cruel visits of the Spanish commissioners, but the humility, misery, and inhumanity they occasioned, are not yet forgotten."

Their periodical visits to see that the treaty obliga-
tions were carried out, were probably used as occasions
for annoying as much as possible those whom they
considered interlopers, and houses were burnt and
plantations demolished by their orders on very slight
pretexts. The high spirit of the Baymen chafed
under this degrading system of inquisition, and when
Don Pedro Ramirez Estios, Governor of Yucatan, and
José Rosado, Comandante of Bacalhal (or Bacalar), by
two letters, dated respectively 29th December, 1763,
and 22nd February, 1764—sent through the "Sergeant
of the Look-Out of St. Anthony," to Joseph Maude,
Esq., chief magistrate [1]—ordered the withdrawal of
all the settlers located on the banks of the Hondo,
they called a public meeting and drew up a petition to
the Governor of Jamaica.

Their memorial was promptly attended to, and the
steps that were taken by our authorities drew from
the Spanish Government a disavowal of the action of
the Governor of Yucatan.

This was probably the first or one of the first acts
incurring a protective relation on the part of the
Government of Jamaica towards the settlement.

On our part, to see that the provisions of the   1765.
last-mentioned treaty were duly executed, the Lords of
the Admiralty appointed Vice-Admiral Sir William
Burnaby to proceed from Port Royal to Honduras, in
1765. The admiral spent nearly a whole year in the
settlement, arranging and settling boundaries, and
placing the settlers in full possession of their locations
and rights.

[1] Almanacs, 1826-29.

He also drew up a code of laws for the settlement, in doing which he was assisted by the celebrated navigator Cook. In the king's name he gave to the people this "constitution," founded on their ancient "forms and usages," a consolidation in fact of their own simple rules of self-government, sanctioned and approved by royal authority. Legislation by public meetings—election of their magistrates by universal suffrage annually—and the control of their finances were preserved to the inhabitants. "Burnaby's Code," as it was ever afterwards known, was the Magna Charta, Bill of Rights, and Habeas Corpus of the settlement of British Honduras.

Vice-Admiral Burnaby's constitution is a thing of the past, but there is no colony of the empire which can boast a more unique system of government than the settlement of British Honduras from its foundation to the appointment of the first representative of royalty —the superintendent. Up to that period, although the colonists' loyalty to the throne has never been impugned, they were so little protected or interfered with, that the crown element was in abeyance practically, and the small community was an instance of government by a pure oligarchy, the governing body elected by an annual *plébiscite*—the public meeting or entire body of inhabitants, exclusive of the slaves. The magistrates, seven in number, prior to the arrival of a superintendent, were responsible to the public meeting alone, and rendered an account, at least of their financial operations, at the expiry of their term of office.

During that term they had entire charge of the

administration of justice, collection and distribution of the revenue, and the appointment of the few necessary officials. Where written law was silent, custom prevailed. The junior magistrate was coroner *ex-officio.*

Robert Hodgson, Esq., was appointed Superintendent of Ruatan. He was dismissed in 1775. **1768.**

War broke out in 1779 between England and Spain. **1779.** The Spanish colonists in Central America had only been waiting a favourable opportunity to recommence their attacks upon the British, whose presence in Honduras was naturally a thorn in their side. Disregarding the agreement to give six months' notice on either part prior to the outbreak of hostilities locally, they took the Baymen unawares at their then principal rendezvous at St. George's Caye.

This island is one of an extended group of coral islets dotting the Bay of Honduras about ten miles from Belize in an easterly direction. To-day it is a mere strip of sand waved over by a few cocoa-nut palms and on which are a few houses, the Caye being still resorted to during certain favourable months of the year as a sanatorium and bathing-place by the wealthier Belizeians. Its former dimensions were probably greater, but have been reduced by the action of the sea, since it was the chief place of the settlement, and seat of government.

The sudden attack of the Spaniards was in this instance successful. Fortunately for some of the settlers, H.M. ships *Badger* and *Racehorse* appeared in the offing, and such as managed to escape were taken on board and to Jamaica ; but the greater number who were not captured, settled in Ruatan, then in occupation by us.[2]

The captives were manacled and marched through the country to Merida, the capital of Yucatan, back again to the coast, and shipped to the Havana, where they were kept in dungeons until July, 1782.

The effect of this attack was to drive a large number of settlers from other parts of the settlement to the Mosquito Shore, and British Honduras as such was hardly in existence for five years after.

1779.   Revenge was taken for this attack on St. George's Caye by the capture of the castle of Omoa by a naval force from Jamaica. The illustrious Nelson took part in the affair, commanding the *Badger* sloop. He subsequently remained some time on the coast to protect the inhabitants, whose thanks he received for his services.

1780.   Omoa was abandoned in the following year, but a more formidable expedition, in which Nelson also shared, was organized, consisting of one line-of-battle ship, two frigates, and two brigs of war, with flats, and a force of two thousand men under Colonel J. Polson. The expedition reached the port of San Juan de Nicaragua on the 24th of March, 1780 ; but the corvette *Henchinbrack*, commanded by young Nelson, was the only vessel that could cross the bar of the river. Lieutenant Nelson ascended the river as far as the island of Mico. The troops were disembarked and reached the fort of San Carlos, which they took, capturing a garrison of 160 men. The Spaniards collected men from

---

[2] Gardiner, in "sketch" in *Honduras Observer*, 7th August, 1847.

San Miguel and elsewhere. The English suffered greatly from the effects of the climate. Great numbers fell sick, and many died. Reinforcements arrived under Captains Dalrymple, Campbell, and Leith, increasing the strength of the expedition to 8000. The *Lord Germain,* armed flat-boat, reached the Lake of Nicaragua, but sickness increasing, and news arriving that further reinforcements on their way had been compelled, owing to an outbreak of typhus fever, to disembark at Kingston, Jamaica, the attempt was finally abandoned, a loss of nearly one half of the force having occurred from the deadly character of the climate. It is probable that the design of this expedition originated in more than a motive of revenge for the successful attack on the British settlement in Honduras at St. George's Caye in 1779 ; and that the intention was to effect a permanent occupation of this region with the object of carrying out the already mooted project of a waterway across this portion of the American continent. Had the result been otherwise than disastrous, the effect upon the settlement whose rise and progress we chronicle might have been to materially alter its history.

In the same year the British were once more dislodged from the island of Ruatan by the Spaniards of Guatemala, and the prisoners carried away to the Havana, to swell the numbers of the captives of 1779.

CHAPTER V.

FROM THE RETURN OF THE SETTLERS AFTER THE CAPTIVITY AT THE HAVANA.

1782-83. THE British Government had no intention of relinquishing the settlement. Its importance had come to be appreciated, at least in certain quarters, as the more explicit terms of the Treaty of Versailles testify.

That treaty was executed on the termination of the American War, and its article vi. contains the following provisions :—

"The intention of the high contracting parties being to prevent, as much as possible, all causes of complaint and misunderstanding heretofore occasioned by the cutting of wood for dyeing, or logwood, and several English settlements having been formed *under that pretence* upon the Spanish Continent, it is expressly agreed that his Britannic Majesty's subjects shall have the right of cutting, loading, and carrying away logwood lying between the River Wallis or Belize and Rio Hondo." The article goes on to secure to the settlers privilege to build the necessary houses and magazines for carrying on their trade, "provided that these stipulations shall not be considered as derogating in any wise from his Catholic Majesty's rights." [1]

In the same year the garrisons at Black River 1782. and Fort Dalling were captured by the Spaniards, who withdrew to Cape Gracias; but a force under Colonel Marcus Despard and Major Laurie retook the positions immediately afterwards.

The liberation of the captives at the Havana was at length effected by the representations of our government in this year. Some few are said to have returned at once to Belize, but the majority went further south to the settlements on the Mosquito Shore, which is a little extraordinary in view of the events occurring in that locality narrated in the preceding paragraph.

Not long after the treaty of 1783 was executed, the settlement began to resume its former appearance.

Commissioners were, in 1784, appointed on either 1784. side to regulate boundaries, and on the 27th of May, in fulfilment of the treaty, formalities were exchanged at the mouth of the New River, Don José Morino Zervallez, "Brigadier of Royal Armies," and Captain-General of the Province of Yucatan, making a formal delivery of the lands to the British Commissioners, Colonel Marcus Despard, Major Richard Hoare, and Captains James McAuly, and Joseph Bartlett— "agreeably to map and instructions I received from my sovereign, having gone over the boundaries and placed proper marks."

Major Hoare, one of the commissioners, remained 1784-85. to arrange the affairs of the settlers who were now

[1] Hertslet, vol. ii. p. 237.

returning to the locations they had been compelled to abandon in 1779. He called a public meeting, which was held for the first time at the "mouth of the Belize River," and not at St. George's Caye. The meeting readopted " Burnaby's Code," and before dissolving appointed the next public assembly for the 1st of October following to be held at the Haulover, where an old fort had been dismantled in accordance with the treaty of 1763.

A characteristic incident was that of the arrival of the *Mercury*, Captain Arnott, from London, with a shipment of convicts purchased from government and brought to Belize for sale. The Baymen would have none of the jail-birds, and calling a special public meeting compelled the captain to take his cargo whence he came or where he chose.

1786-87.　The colony would now appear to have reattained its position previous to the disaster of 1779. From vol. ii. of Hertslet, page 247, we learn that on the 14th of July, 1786, additional articles were added by the Convention of London to the treaty of 1783, granting more extended boundaries to the south. "The Catholic king" wishing "to prove, on his side, to the king of Great Britain, the sincerity of his sentiments of friendship towards his Majesty and the British nation."

The English line now began from the sea, and, taking the centre, proceeded up the Sibun (Sherboon or Javon) River to its source, then across to the intersection of the River Wallis (Belize), thus adding nine miles of coast-line to the settlement.[2]

[2] Art. ii., Convention of London, 1786.

The right of cutting not dyewoods only, but, for the first time, "not excepting even mahogany," was granted by article iii., and also permission to gather the fruits of the earth purely natural; but the same article expressly stipulates that this grant is to be no pretext for establishing any plantations of "sugar, coffee, cocoa, or other like articles," mills, or machines, and reserves as usual sovereign rights to the crown of Spain, which are also again reserved in article vii. of the same convention.

The treaty of 1783 required the evacuation by the British of the Mosquito Shore. The settlers from Black River, and other positions on that disputed territory, with their families and slaves, were brought to Belize by the British Government, and among them were the remainder of the captives liberated from the dungeons of the Havana, who had preferred the Shore to an immediate return to Honduras, when set free in 1782. This accession swelled the number of the inhabitants to something like former times. A document of the period, dated the 4th of August, 1786, is signed by 112 persons.

On the 27th of June of that year the work of reconstruction was completed by the holding of another public meeting, over which the first superintendent, Colonel Edward Marcus Despard, presided. Their labours were confined to judicial arrangements, continued from time to time by a committee of seven, who regulated also customs and harbour-dues. Colonel Despard fixed his residence at the chief military station, the Haulover. Col. Despard, 1st Superintendent.

The town of Belize was planned, regulated, and

enlarged, and the public meetings were then first held at the " Court House, Belize Point."

St. George's Caye has been previously described as the chief place of the settlement—the principal resort of the wealthier inhabitants in former days for public business and private retirement, when not engaged in " cutting, loading, and carrying away " their timber. But from 1738 to 1765 there sprang up a town at the mouth of the Belize, especially on the delta formed by its double embouchure. Stoccadoed buildings were in existence, and a fort at the other outlet of the river, the Haulover; and from Belize Point, as well as other points in the settlement, wood was shipped.

1787.   In 1787 the mere nucleus of a town had as yet been formed. In this year it was laid out in lots, 50 feet by 100 feet, and these lots were balloted for, the lots being taken up chiefly by those who had recently returned or newly arrived from Ruatan and the Mosquito Coast.

The work of reconstruction thus completed may be looked upon as the foundation of the present colony. But, unfortunately, a terrible hurricane visited the settlement. Valuable property was injured and lives lost. Every house in the settlement was destroyed except one. The houses, however, at this period, it must be remembered, were unsubstantial erections of wood, thatched with the leaf of a species of palm. This thatch is still known as " bay-leaf." As Honduras is out of the ordinary track of these tropical storms, it has been but rarely that it has suffered from a visitation of this kind which has done similar damage.

Colonel Despard, the first superintendent, found his new government by no means a sinecure.

Dissensions were rife; and he was soon embroiled with the high-spirited Baymen, unused to the novelty of a representative of royalty dwelling in their midst. They were loyal in their sentiments and conduct, but fondly attached to their primitive oligarchy and its simple rules of administration.

The constitution of the settlement now lost its unique character, and assumed an anomalous one. The oligarchical element was preserved in the retention of legislation by the public meeting, and the annual election of magistrates, who continued to control the finances, and to administer justice; but the monarchical principle was introduced—visibly now—in the person of the superintendent, appointed from Jamaica, but probably nominated, or at all events approved of, at home.[3]

That the two political elements should frequently clash was what was perhaps to be expected. The superintendent was closely watched by the magisterial body, and they were as closely supervised by the executive, and irritated by a control new and unaccustomed. Financial and legislative measures were

---

[3] The Governor of Jamaica was styled in his commission Captain-General of Jamaica and the territories thereon depending in America, *i.e.* the Mosquito Shore and British Honduras. "But his jurisdiction over these settlements having been imperfectly defined, was seldom acknowledged by the settlers; except when they wished to plead it in bar of the authority claimed by their respective superintendents."—"History of the West Indies," by Bryan Edwards, London, 1793, vol. i. p. 124.

E

initiated on both sides, to fall to the ground through the opposition of one or other.

The admission of Spanish commissioners, who twice a year came to "examine into the real situation of things"—that no forts or fortifications of any kind were erected, the limits assigned for the cutting of mahogany and dyewood were not exceeded, and no plantations, beyond a certain extent, were formed, nor any particular mode of culture pursued [4]—as has been already recorded, was particularly annoying to the inhabitants, whose easily-roused spirit and ancient hostility—revived by recent events—towards the South American Spaniards required little to excite it to action. When, therefore, in 1789 Colonel Despard, urged by complaints made by the Spanish authorities that the jurisdiction of the court of magistrates was an infringement of the article vii. of the Convention of London of 1786, and derogatory from the sovereign rights of the king of Spain, sought to introduce a change in the legislative and judicial system, his proceedings were strenuously opposed, and confusion and discord—anarchy almost—took the place of the customary peaceful tenor of the internal affairs of the community. The superintendent was not without a few interested supporters, who probably misled him as to the true sentiments of the majority of the inhabitants.

It is impossible, without adequate materials to ground one upon, to pass any opinion definitely as to the dispute; but it is reasonable to infer that the first superintendent was injudicious in forcing upon the Baymen further changes in the constitution to which

1789.

[4] Captain Henderson's account, 1809.

they were attached, before they had had time even to become in some measure used to the alteration which had just taken place in his own appointment. But the superintendent had received a military training, and may probably have looked upon the settlers as still a band of adventurers on Spanish lands, descendants or successors of lawless, piratical freebooters, who had not acquired their footing on the Main in the regular way either of peaceful colonization or legitimate military conquest. Let these matters be how they may, " Burnaby's Code " was loudly demanded by the inhabitants.

The questions at issue between them and the executive were eventually referred, and the result was in favour of the settlers. In the following year, Colonel Peter Hunter arrived to relieve Colonel Despard as superintendent, and a proclamation was at once issued restoring its ancient laws to the settlement, as fixed by Burnaby's Code, and calling a public meeting to be held at " Mrs. Hodge's Tavern, North Side," at which a new magistracy on the old plan was returned, and peace again reigned. *1790. Colonel Hunter, Superin- tendent.*

Colonel Hunter returned to Jamaica, leaving the the affairs of the settlement once more in the hands of the magistrates. To those in office at the moment of his departure, he gave certain instructions for their guidance, and confirmed the constitution by " an express sanction of his Majesty to it." *1791-96. Govern- ment of Magis- trates.*

Since the incident of Colonel Despard's innovations, in consequence of their representations, the periodical visitations of Spanish Commissioners had been discontinued; but in the year 1791 great uneasiness pervaded the community on account of the attitude of the

Spanish colonists in Yucatan, from the probability of their pressing similar demands to those to which Colonel Despard had yielded, by force. There were no adequate means of defence, and, deprived of the superintendent and commander-in-chief, they were without a superior military officer of experience to organize any. Application was made to Jamaica, for another superintendent and commander-in-chief.

The practice of the African superstition of Obeah was made a capital offence. Its occult rites had been introduced by slaves from the other colonies; and its incantations, potions, and general mumbo-jumboism, are looked upon with a kind of reverent dread, little short of awe and terror, by the descendants of the slaves in the present day.

1795.　It was found necessary to institute a guard to control the slaves during the annual Christmas holidays, the different African tribes, no doubt, occasionally indulging in faction-fights. This was probably the nucleus of the " Prince Regent's Royal Regiment of Militia."

1796.　Ruatan, left a neglected desert by the Spaniards, was reoccupied by the British as a penal settlement for Caribs.

Col. Barrow, Superintendent.　The increased warlike attitude of the Spaniards induced the inhabitants of British Honduras to make further representations, which resulted in their wishes being acceded to; and the appointment of Colonel Barrow as civil superintendent and military commandant " to command his Majesty's subjects armed, or that were to be armed."

On their own part the inhabitants had laid in a

supply of defensive weapons for themselves, and had also armed their slaves with pikes. It is a fact worthy of note, that, almost from their introduction, the slaves on the mahogany works of Honduras have been permitted to carry weapons without any untoward results to their masters on a single occasion, but that they have uniformly used them with good effect in defence of these same masters. The machéte, the implement used in clearing the bush, hangs always by their side, and though a cutlass of formidable shape in their muscular arms, it has never been put to a bad use in that way.

The hostile attitude of their neighbours beyond their limits, the prohibition to erect any defensive works of a permanent character, and the disinclination of the home government or of the authorities in Jamaica to afford them continuous military protection, led, early in 1797, to the assembling of a public meeting to deliberate, " Whether this meeting do consider it most for the interests of the community at large to continue to carry on defensive operations for keeping possession of the settlement, or to determine upon a general evacuation.'' The question was keenly debated, and the *dernier ressort* of evacuation was only prevented being carried by fourteen votes. 1797

"THE PORK AND DOUGH BOYS' WAR."

This year must ever be considered as memorable in the annals of British Honduras. To the events of that year it refers its final consolidation and legitimate recognition as a settlement or colonial fragment of the British Empire; its limits having been there 1798. Martial Law.

and then determined by right of undoubted conquest,
no longer resting upon treaty boundaries with Spain,
nor its existence for the future amounting to a mere
tolerated occupation for special purposes.   The second
engagement at St. George's Caye was its Bannockburn;
and, says the present colonial secretary, the Hon.
Henry Fowler, in a slight historical sketch appended
to his interesting "Narrative of a Journey across
the unexplored portion of British Honduras, 1879 :"
"Few colonies can boast a history so unique or
thrilling, or give such a proof of the dogged tenacity
of the English race."

The Yucatecan ports of Bacalar and Campeché were
busy during the early portion of the year 1798 with
the preparations for an attack upon the settlement on
a large scale.   The British were to be driven from the
territory of Spain once and for all.   The Baymen were
not without warning, however, of these warlike preparations, or themselves unprepared to meet the im-
pending attack.   The only thing was to ascertain in
what direction to look to anticipate it ; a struggle for
life and for their homes they knew was before them.
It is easy to imagine the excitement that must have
seized the little community, the suspense they must
have endured.   It is not possible to exaggerate the
courage and calm resolution of the small band of inhabitants, which sustained them to await the onset
from whatever quarter it might come, rather than re-
consider their former decision, and, in face of the dan-
gers around them, adopt total evacuation in preference
to a life and death struggle.

Armed, as we have already stated, themselves and

slaves, but indifferently, and supported only by the gunboat *Merlin*, they collected at St. George's Caye flat-bottomed logwood-lighters, mounted guns in them, and stationed them along the shoals. H.M.S. *Merlin*, 8-gun brig, Captain Moss, took up her station off St. George's Caye, and as many coasting-vessels as could be got together were manned and armed. For months the scouting doreys, quick sailers, were out at sea to warn them of the approach of the enemy, while a watch was kept from the land side.

About the 4th to the 8th of September, the scouts at sea reported a large naval force approaching, and the Spanish fleet could soon be made out from the mast-head of the *Merlin* as it made Caye Chappel. The Baymen promptly burned their houses on St. George's, having previously removed their families and valuables to spots less exposed, and prepared to do or die.

The Spanish fleet, commanded by Captain Boca Negra, consisted of fourteen sail of the line and a flotilla of flat-bottomed boats; a total of vessels amounting to thirty-two of all rigs and sizes. Nine vessels, and the boats, engaged in the attack; five were held in reserve. A force of 3000 of all arms accompanied this fleet, and the expedition was under the orders of General O'Noil, a field-marshal of Spain, who was then Governor and Captain-General of Yucatan. The Spaniards attempted to force a passage over the Montego Shoals, with six of the heaviest vessels. The Belize force is thus given by H. Gardiner in the sketch of Honduras written by him for the *Honduras Observer*, August 7th, 1847. Besides H.M.S. *Merlin*, there were two sloops with one 18-pounder each, and

twenty-five men; two schooners with one 6-pounder
each, and twenty-five men; seven gun-flats with one
9-pounder each, and sixteen men. Colonel Barrow
defended the Haulover with 200 men, including detach-
ments of the 6th West India and 63rd Regiments, and
of the Royal Artillery.

The engagement began on the 10th, Captain Moss
in the *Merlin* securing St. George's Caye at the
instant the Spaniards, with twelve of their vessels,
attempted to capture it. They thereupon (the
Spaniards) hauled their wind for Long Caye, and
then bore down—nine sail of sloops and schooners
carrying from twelve to twenty guns, including ten
24 and 18-pounders in the bow and stern of each—
upon the Belize flotilla. The contest lasted off and
on for two days, during which the most determined
bravery was displayed by the defenders. A steady
and well-directed fire was kept up from the flats stationed on the shoals, the coasting-vessels, and by the
Merlin, and the result was that the Spaniards fell back
on their reserves. A high meed of praise is due to
the gallant defenders, but it does not detract there-
from to draw the necessary inference that, had so
superior a force not been impeded by the nature of
the waters in which the engagement took place—a
circumstance also much in favour of the defence—it is
impossible but that the invasion would have had a
different termination. The execution done on the
crowded decks of the Spanish vessels by the steady,
well-managed fire from the home flotilla, reflects the
highest credit on the skill and courage of all concerned
in repulsing the attack, and this the Earl of Balcarres

acknowledged on the part of the king in a despatch to Colonel Barrow,[*] through the Governor of Jamaica. The Spaniards' local Armada went off with a light southerly wind to Bacalar and Campeché, and thus the last attempt to dispossess the settlers terminated. Since then the crown of Spain has renewed and confirmed old treaties and privileges, but tacitly acknowledged the right of the settlers to the territory they had now won on the same terms as those upon which Spain herself acquired all the American possessions—legitimate conquest. The independent states of Central America have never shown an inclination to disturb the peace of the settlement, but trade and commerce has sprung up between us and all of them. Since September, 1798, with the exception of inroads on the northern frontier by plunder-seeking bands of semi-civilized Mayas, the colony has been free from attack. The limits of the colony were extended to the River Sarstoon, which has remained the most southern boundary.

The "Pork and Dough Boys'" war is the local name given to the encounter, from the fact that salt pork and "Johnny cakes," or cakes of a doughy consistency seasoned by fat pork, is the staple diet of the Honduras wood-cutter. Others make it "Poke and Do," from the Palmetto pikes handled so well by them against the Dons; but "poke and do" is the natural corruption in the Creole dialect for "pork and dough."

1779 was devoted to putting things to rights. Number of magistrates restored from five to seven.

[*] Honourably mentioned, J. Paslow, Esq., and slaves.

CHAPTER VI.

DESCRIPTION.

THE limits of the colony having now been determined definitely upon the boundary-lines which are found existing at the present time, it may be the appropriate place to give its geographical outlines and topography.

Geographical situation.

It forms, in point of fact, an integral portion of the former kingdom of Guatemala, its northern extremity projecting into Yucatan, its southern resting on Spanish Honduras, and the present Republic of Guatemala forming its western frontier. It lies between 15° 53′ 55″ and 18° 29′ 5″ north latitude, and between 18° 10′ and 89° 9′ 92″ west longitude. Its extreme length is about 180 or 190 miles, and its average depth from the coast-line to the western frontier, forty to forty-five miles. The northern boundary is the Rio Hondo, the southern the River Sarstoon. By a convention with the Republican Government of Guatemala, determined by Major Ray, R.E, in 1860, the western boundary is fixed by a line drawn from the head of the Hondo and passing through Garbutt's Falls to a point on the Sarstoon. The Bay or Gulf of Honduras is numerously studded by islands and protected by a long line of coralline reef. Area, 6250 miles—4,000,000 acres.

The coast-line fronting the bay, after a deep in- Coast-line. dentation to the mouth of the New River, runs boldly out in the promontory of Rocky Point for about eighteen miles, and when this headland is rounded, continues in an uninterrupted line of coast due south for 160 miles to the southern limit.

The entire seaboard is protected, as above stated, by the parallel line of reefs running north and south at a distance of about ten miles from the main land, forming a natural breakwater, and rendering navigation of the coast safe for vessels of light draught; but for 100 miles to the south of Belize there is a depth of three fathoms' soundings close in shore.

The district is intersected by numerous rivers, all Rivers. navigable for craft of light draught. The Hondo and New River run almost due north, trending east a little from their source. The Northern River has a short course due east from Cutter's Lagoon to the sea. The centre of the region is watered by the Old or Belize River and its tributary streams. Its course is very tortuous, first running north from its rise and then winding east and south to the coast. The remaining streams flow eastward from the interior—the Sibun, Sittee, Manatee, Sarstoon, and Mullins River, some of them taking their rise in a spur of the Cockscomb Mountains. The River Belize, from its embouchure at the town of Belize to the fork or "branch," allowing for sinuosities, is estimated at 150 miles—75 miles with the crow. The breadth at "Orange Walk" is 187 feet; depth, 3 feet, 6 feet,

9 feet, 6 feet, 3 feet, at different points across. At the Haulover, or upper outlet to the sea, it is 600 feet, and 10 feet deep. At Belize Bridge it is 121 feet by 8 feet, 11 feet, 6 feet, the depths across.

NAVIGABLE DISTANCE UP THE SEVERAL RIVERS.

Hondo, navigable from its bar towards source . 60 miles.
New River ,,   ,,   ,, . 60 ,,
Old River ,,   ,,   ,, . 120 ,,
Sibun   ,,   ,,   ,, . 30 ,,
Manatee ,,   ,,   ,, . 16 ,,
Mullins ,,   ,,   ,, . 16 ,,
Sittee   ,,   ,,   ,, . 16 ,,
North Stann Creek ,,   ,, . 18 ,,
Sarstoon, navigable ,,   ,, . 10 ,,
The smaller rivers for a few miles—all of them.[1]

The water at the flood rises in some places twenty, thirty-five, and forty feet in the main river, and in the creeks ten and twenty feet. The following elevations are deduced from barometrical observations made by the late Samuel Cockburn, Esq., police-magistrate of the settlement, a native of one of the West Indian islands, who made geology and meteorology his studious recreations :—

Point on Belize River.	Distance from mouths.	Height from sea-level to water's edge.	Height from sea-level to top of bank.	Height from level of stream to top of bank.
Orange Walk	90 miles	32 feet.	60 feet.	28 feet.
Young Gal's Bank	93 ,,	34 ,, 6 in.	68 ,, 10 in.	34 ,,
Mount Hope	100 ,,	172 ,, 3 ,,	207 ,, 10 ,,	35 ,, 7 in.
Between "Spanish Look Out" and Duck Run	106 ,,	173 ,,	242 ,,	69 ,, 7 ,,

[1] Honduras Almanac, W. G. Wilson, 1880.

The hydrographic basin of the northern portion of the Belize River district is much lower than the river itself. Consequently, in the rainy season, much of the country is under water. The creeks and lagoons, their waters pushed back by the main-river flood, overflow and inundate the valleys between the intervening ridges or elevated lands. But, according to Mr. Cockburn, "The lands are slowly rising as much from the detritus brought down by the river as from the gentle influence of internal forces, and, in the course of time, even the lagoons will silt up and become dry, so that in afterages the whole will become a rich bottom, covered with alluvial deposits of the most productive kind, in the same manner as the existing ridges were before they were elevated to their present height. As the river is ascended, the banks on either side rise in a gentle acclivity. The limestone formation crops out here and there, embedded in a concretion of coarse calcareous grit, mixed with iron oxide, silicates, and feldspathic breccia, covered with thick layers of marl, loam, and clay, and overtopped by silt and detritus of the river. The formation about the Old River may be described as a marine limestone of the tertiary period. The sand of the river indicates, under the microscope, particles of granite, basalt, and other igneous rock, mica, feldspar, and iron pyrites. These are, of course, not *in situ*, but the result of rain-washings, and transported by the river from beds of conglomerate in the interior, and the disintegrated sides of mountains. The formation is undoubtedly a marine limestone of the tertiary period, but of a soft, coarse, and impure description, more of a sort of calcareous breccia, in some places not unlike the *calcaire grossier* of the Paris basin, and so recent, geologically speaking, as hardly yet to have acquired a consistency beyond indurated calcareous marl." [2]

Fragments of shells procured by Mr. Cockburn at Young Gal Bank, ninety-three miles from the sea, find their analogues in existing species of *volutæ* obtained in the waters of the neighbouring bay— showing how very recent the formation is, probably "posterior to the pleistocene of the tertiary."

The banks of the river, except at the clearings, are clothed with the dense foliage of the prickly bamboo, and some distance up, the river is obstructed by shoals and rapids. River craft of light draught, such as pit- pans or flat-bottomed canoes, navigate its whole course, and there are numerous clearings or "banks" from the mouth to the source at intervals. Logwood is brought down in canoes or "bark logs," and mahogany floated down almost from the source, when there is a sufficiently high flood. As yet the cultivation at the "banks" is limited. The land is undulating, rising in a gentle slope of cahoon and pine-ridges up to the base of the Blue Mountains of Guatemala. The entire population of the Old River district may be roughly estimated at ten thousand.

The prevailing type of formation for the whole colony is tertiary. The soil is a varying depth of clayey loam, overtopped with rich black mould and a subsoil of calcareous marl, the pine-ridges having a layer of sand. It does not appear that the laminated formation of limestone extends to the cayes or islands

[2] Cockburn, "Rough Notes," 1867-69.

which group themselves at various distances from the main throughout the bay, but that these are accumulations of river-silt and detritus, covered with sand and overgrown with mangrove-bush; some remaining perfectly submerged while others are more solid. The waters around them abound in fish and crustacea, mollusca, radiata, sponges, sea-fans, pumice-stone, and fusi and algæ. Near the mainland the floor of the sea is covered with soft mud, to seaward it is fine calcareous sand.

For a few miles inwards from the coast, the country is low and swampy, abounding in profuse vegetation and with numerous lagoons. The swamps and lagoons are thickly grown with the mangrove (*rhizophora mangle*) of which there are three varieties, the red, white, and black; manchineel (*hippomane mancinella*), poponax, and button-wood, &c., &c. As we ascend the rivers, however, we find ourselves encompassed by lofty banks consisting of alluvial deposits, and at moderate distances from the rivers are the "pine-ridges," so familiar to the inhabitants of the southern states of North America.

Towards the western, and particularly the south-western boundary, the region developes table-lands and plateaux. The range of mountains beginning at Sibun and running nearly parallel to the coast, are clothed with verdure to their summits, but at right angles to these are others veiled in mist rising behind, higher and higher, in amphitheatrical form, whose conical peaks proclaim their volcanic birth. The highest point is in the Cockscomb, 4000 feet of elevation.

The whole coast from Sibun to Sarstoon, 103 miles, is intersected by the rivers already enumerated and many smaller creeks. The rivers rising in the hills have short runs to the sea, and are navigable for smaller vessels some distance from their mouths. In most places the shore is still marshy and covered with vegetation, but there are numerous strips of sandy beaches, as for example, Stann Creek, Punta Gorda, and Commerce Bight, upon which the Caribs build their villages, and where the land slopes gently inwards and the streams run over pebbles and clean brown sand. Such strips, sometimes of considerable extent, are admirably adapted for cocoa-nut walks, behind them there is alluvial land for ranchos and plantations, and only requiring to be approached and opened up; behind that, again, the mountain-slopes and hill-sides suitable for coffee and cacoa.

The formation is regularly stratified, and consists of indurated argillaceous limestone (Cockburn) in laminæ between thin beds of fine clay; superstratum, clayey loam of varying thickness; top-dressing of rich black mould with sand on the pine and cahoon ridges.

Probably, the most valuable districts are these cahoon-ridges, in which abound cedar and mahogany, and the cahoon-palm, valuable on account of the oil to be extracted from its nuts. The soil of these ridges is richest virgin. They occupy two-fifths of the area of the colony, and are scattered over it, varying in size from a quarter of a mile wide to twelve and twenty miles square; some situated near the coast, others in the heart of the country.

As the washings from the hills in the southern

portion of the colony will give a constant supply of carbonates, silicates, and the phosphates arising from the decomposition of the limestone, the lands in that district will remain fertile, and will produce over and over again crops such as sugar-cane without becoming exhausted. Increased attention to agriculture must in time fill up the thinly-populated district of the south, most of which, with the exception of a few large and a few small sugar estates, is left to Caribs.

South Snake Caye was (1867) an example of the palpable operations of the tiny coral insects in their labour of construction, which an attentive observer could discern for himself. The stalactite caves of Manatee are objects of curiosity. There are others at Indian Creek on the Sibun, described by Captain Henderson as "sublime."

The northern district, or that portion of the colony the correct southern boundary of which is Northern River, is a dead flat, with the exception of a few small hillocks or ridges, and some shallow basins with a very gentle incline from the western frontier to the sea—a plain of about one thousand square miles. There are several lagoons, but comparatively few swamps. The soil is a vegetable mould (*humus*) some twelve or eighteen inches deep, subsoil stony marl. Sinking wells at Corozal, the principal place in the district, madrepores have been found at a depth of thirty feet, and more recently a bed of fossil oysters was come upon at Caledonia, on New River, seventeen feet below the surface. *Northern district.*

The New River, flowing in a north-westerly direction from its source, in the same watershed as the Old *New River.*

F

River, near the centre of the western frontier, is the principal highway for travel up country. It runs from the lagoon at Indian Church down to the bight at Corozal (Rowley's Bight), and its course is exactly parallel with the Rio Hondo (which forms the north and north-western boundary of the colony) ; for some seventy miles navigable for small craft. It is a dull, sluggish stream, without rapids, and never overflows, consequently the alluvium on its banks cannot compare with the deposits on the margins of the other rivers to the south.

Northern River. Northern River is a short stream by which a lagoon empties itself into the sea. It is encompassed by rich land.

The Hondo. The Hondo, as its name signifies, is the deepest river in the settlement. Its lower bank has been occupied by us from an early date of the settlement for fifty miles up. Large vessels not drawing too much water—like the Spanish bungays—navigate it for a considerable distance from the mouth.

The Sibun. All the rivers have bars at their entrance, which are very obstructive to navigation. The source of the Sibun is not yet determined. British settlers occupy it for 120 miles of its course. The left branch near the source disappears for some distance in the sand. It is perhaps the river whose banks are most diversified of all those the colony boasts, and at points the scenery loses the monotonous character of the other riverain regions, and becomes picturesque. It is only navigable, except for small canoes, a short distance up ; and although its banks are said to be lined with good wood, it is next to an impossibility to get the logs out.

The district is mountainous, and the flood rises and falls very suddenly.

That portion of the colony lying between the Hondo and a line drawn from Belize to Indian Church, embraces a region the formation of which consists of thin surface-soil, the decayed droppings of trees over a sub-soil of indurated marl. The uplands are so far interior that very little of their *débris* reaches this district, unlike the southern, in which the surface-soil is alluvial from the greater contiguity of high lands. At Indian Church the limestone crops up, and beyond the Hondo the Yu-catecan hills arise. To the west, about Booth's River, the Bravo, and the Blue Creek (tributaries of the Hondo), the marl has a top soil of blue clay under the surface-soil. The absence of alluvium and detritus in the northern district is manifestly owing to the slower currents of the rivers.

This district is more populous than that lying to the Towns: south of the Sibun. Corozal is, properly speaking, an Corozal. Indian or Yucatecan town, with a population of be-tween two and three thousand, and has several sugar-ranchos in its neighbourhood. It lies in the bight beyond Rocky Point, close to New River mouth. It can never be a place of much importance commercially, not being approachable by large vessels from sea, but it may and probably will become an agricultural centre and depôt for a bartering kind of trade with Yucatan. Further up the New River are the villages of Orange Walk[4] and San Estevan, similar in character to Corozal, and differing only in size and population.

[4] There are New River Orange Walk and Old River Orange Walk.

The district of Corozal and New River, as far as the Hondo boundary, is dotted with "ranchos" and "milpas," upon which sugar, corn (maize), rice, ground provisions, and fruits, are raised.

Ambergris Caye, a large island opposite the northern portion of the coast-line, is very suitable for settlement and agriculture. It is at present thinly populated.

Towns, &c. continued. The southern district has no towns, and little else beyond Carib villages, and the houses of the labourers on the several sugar estates carried on in the district.

The town of Belize, viewed from the harbour, is extremely pretty; its jalousied, chimneyless houses, and public buildings, churches, assembly-rooms, court-house, &c., nestling among the palms and oleanders; the mountains to the south in the hazy distance; the distant cayes looming out to sea, those closer looking brightly green in the noonday sun; and the harbour enlivened by shipping of all rigs and sizes. It is built on the banks of the river for about half a mile up, and sweeps north and south along the shore from the mouth of the river. The river is spanned by a neat and substantial bridge, one originally constructed in 1797, rebuilt higher up in 1816-18, and the present one completed and opened in 1859.

The northern half of the town is built on an island or delta formed by the double embouchure of the river. There are the barracks (Newtown), the public hospital, and jail (brick-built,) the Belize Estate Company's (formerly the British Honduras Company) buildings and "barquedier," St. Mary's church, Baptist, and second Wesleyan chapel, and Roman Catholic church.

In the centre of the town, one of the most enterprising merchants, Mr. C. T. Hunter, has erected a brick house three storeys high, regardless of earthquakes. On the south side are the court-house, finished in 1880 (the former building was pulled down in 1878, having lasted since 1819, and the mahogany logs dug from its foundation were found in as good " heart " as they were when laid down), the house of assembly, government-house, and a handsome Wesleyan chapel of brick. St. John's Church (1812) is also built of brick. The town is kept very clean, and has a decent market, several handsome stores and commodious private dwellings. Population of the colony by the census of 1881: white, 375; coloured, 27,077; total, 27,452.

Beyond the natural waterways of the region, the internal communications of the colony are in a very backward state. Outside the towns and villages there is nothing worthy the name of a road; one is in course of construction from Belize, by the present disgraceful Haulover road, to Peten, but the course selected for it is the subject of much dispute, and it is doubtful if, when finished, it will prove of advantage to the colony. At present, travellers into the interior are condemned to follow mere bush-tracks and mahogany truck-paths, or resort to the picturesque pitpan, or historical canoe of the days of Bartolomé Columbus. The importance of the improvement in internal communications towards the development of the colony cannot be exaggerated.

The sculptured and hieroglyphic remains of Mexico, Guatemala, and Yucatan, are not to be found within *Archæology.*

the limits of British Honduras, but the Indian tumuli, akin to the " barrows " of Great Britain and European continental countries, yield earthenware and stone relics, and human remains. These tumuli are found about the banks of the rivers.

CHAPTER VII.

" VALOROUS enterprise, a manly, noble, and laudably ambitious daring, first gave the settlers a footing from the shores of Campeché to Cape Gracias á Dios, and the same indomitable perseverance and indefatigable pursuit after wealth, under circumstances of difficulty and danger, have given them the most unexceptionable right to the very small portion of Honduras which they now possess." So writes Mr. Henry Gardiner of Belize, in the *Honduras Observer* of the 7th of August, 1847, with reasonable pride in the colony of which he was an inhabitant; and we fancy all who have followed our imperfect record of its early history will coincide with him. Although forming an integral portion of the Spanish conquests in America geographically, British Honduras never politically belonged to Spain, was never occupied by Spaniards, but was found by the British in possession of Indian tribes. In fact, Yucatan itself has never been entirely conquered by the Spaniards, and the " guerra de castas " is continued to-day from the time of Grijalva and Montejo.

Up to the point at which we have arrived, the record

of the early settlement of the region is one of continuous struggle against not only hostile and jealous
neighbours, but against the rugged aspect nature
presents in these climes, dense jungle, tempestuous
weather, and—to toil in—a trying climate. That
struggle had been manfully sustained by the Baymen,
and now, from the opening of the present century, the
history becomes one of peaceful progress, advance in
civilization, and improvement in social characteristics
and political institutions.

1800.
Colonel
Barrow
Superin-
tendent to
August,
1800.

The period from 1800 to 1830 may be looked upon
as the halcyon days of the settlement. Internal peace
was chequered by the perhaps wholesome excitement
of constitutional changes, but exempt from external
attack. At each alteration made in their "ancient
usages and customs," the spirited Baymen and back-
woodsmen chafed, and roused themselves whenever an
injudicious superintendent or law-official pulled too
hard on the curb; but in the long-run they proved
themselves consistently a loyal, law-abiding community.

During the first decade of the present century,
England was engaged in the Napoleonic war: it was
therefore hardly to be looked for, while Wellington
was at the head of combined forces of Englishmen and
Spaniards, driving the French out of the Peninsula,
that the Spanish colonists should renew their attempts
to expel British subjects from land now theirs by
conquest. For years to come the settlers enjoyed
immunity from foreign aggression.

1801.
Sir B. Bas-
set, Supt.

In the year above named they established a currency
in which fines were made payable, instead of in logwood.

About this time, the Governor of Jamaica, Colonel Nugent, sent a Captain Corbett to Honduras to report upon its capabilities.[1] He remained some time, and ascended both the Belize and Sibun Rivers. His report if he made any, has not seen the light, nor produced any visible result.

August, 1800-1802. Captains Leeson and McDonald, *ad interim.*

The first permanent fortification was constructed on an island, formed principally of English soil, discharged as ballast, on the north side of the river-mouth. It was named Fort George. Duty first imposed on imported liquors.

1803. Colonel Barrow Supt. 1804. Colonel Gordon, Supt.

In the year following, Colonel Gordon was succeeded by Colonel Mark Kerr Hamilton. Proper regulations for slave courts were drawn up, and these courts placed on a right footing.

1805. Colonel Hamilton. Superintendent.

Intercourse of an amicable character appears at this time to have been carried on between the authorities of Belize and Merida (Yucatan), by means of Indian couriers.

1806.

According to Captain Henderson, an officer of the 5th West India Regiment stationed at Belize about this time, who was officially sent on a mission to Mosquitia, and who has written a short account[2] of Honduras and his trip to the Mosquito Coast, 1806, the then Captain-General of Yucatan was a generally esteemed, amiable Spanish gentleman.

From the same authority we learn that the population then was 200 pure whites, 500 free persons of colour, and 3000 slaves, but no census had been recently taken. According to more definite statistics from other sources, we take the three years—

[1] Henderson.   [2] London, 1809.

1802.	Free .	.	.	.	735
	Slaves		.	.	2146
	Total	.	.	.	2881

1803.	Total	.	.	.	3500

1805.	Free .	.	.	.	1098
	Slaves		.	.	2540
	Total	.	.	.	3638

The revenue was at this time about 6000*l.* to 7000*l.* annually, derived from the tonnage and harbour-dues (3*l.* on each ship), duties, fines, licences, and a tax on transient traders. Dry goods, cutlery, glassware and crockery, and salt meat, were imported from Europe; flour, salt pork and fish, potatoes, and provisions generally, from America. Upon mahogany shipped to the United States, both from Jamaica and Honduras, there was a restriction as to the size of the logs. The following is a statement of wood shipped in the years 1802-5, from newspaper reports:—

Year.	Mahogany.	Logwood.
	Feet.	Tons.
1802	2,125,000	698
1803	4,500,000	900
1804	6,481,000	1412
1805	2,434,000	1268

No reason is assigned for the falling off in 1805. As cattle were now beginning to be used in the wood-cutting operations, a trade with the south and the interior sprang up in cattle and mules for use in trucking-out, and this was also, probably, the beginning of a reciprocal business in general merchandize, which eventually led to the port of Belize becoming a depôt for European and American manufactures.

Twice a year application was made to Jamaica for a convoy for the Honduras merchant fleet.

Henderson alludes to the great wealth of the free inhabitants, white and coloured, in his time. The latter class were slave-owners as well as the whites.

He also remarks that the slaves of Honduras possessed "indulgences not granted to their condition in any other country." According to the same authority, the value of a slave on importation was 120*l.* to 160*l.* currency ; when trained, his value increased to 200*l.* and 300*l.* The annual cost of a slave (he estimates in detail) amounted to 25*l.* to 30*l.* a year. Saturday was the slave's own to employ as he liked, but his owner allowed him 3*s.* 4*d.* currency, for every Saturday he worked for him. The slaves' rations on mahogany work were five pounds of pork and seven pounds of flour, with sugar and tobacco—the same as to-day, less the luxuries. The arrangements for domestics were of course different, but all slaves were housed and clad, as well as fed by their masters. At Christmas, when the season's work of cutting, hauling, manufacturing and bringing out was over, the slaves were allowed from three weeks' to a month's licence to enjoy the pleasures of town in Belize, according to the respective ideas of what was enjoyment peculiar to the several tribes. These congregated in separate bodies, and followed the African rites they had brought with them, but all displaying the same wonderful endurance in undergoing the fatigues of dissipation that they undoubtedly did in sustaining those of toil—" keeping it up " day and night. Amongst other questionable results deducible from slavery-times, this of keeping festivity going all night as well as all day, clings to the celebration of the Christmas holiday still. Music and dancing and the extravagant consumption of gunpowder by discharging it from their shot-guns, were common to all the tribes. Pitpan-races on the river formed a much more interesting and agreeable feature of the carnival, and a prettier aquatic sight cannot be witnessed in any quarter of the globe.

The mahogany pitpan is a long, narrow " dug-out," drawing only a few inches of water in the centre, rising to square ends bow and stern, and peculiarly adapted for river navigation, in which of all sizes it is employed to transport supplies from Belize to the works up-river, and logwood from thence to Belize. In antiquity it probably yields to no known specimen of naval architecture, having been found in use among the aboriginal tribes at the Spanish discovery of this part of America. Some of them are fitted with permanent awnings in the middle, rather aft.

On race-days the largest pitpans are manned by crews of from twenty to forty paddlers, appropriately dressed and representing rival mahogany firms. The crew is placed forward, the steersman right aft, guiding the craft with the utmost nicety by a light stroke of his paddle, or a peculiar turn or twist of its blade in the water. The crews keep excellent time, the thirty or forty hands clutching the notch in the top of the paddle, rising in the air together as if moved by machinery, with a one-two, or a one-two-three stroke as the leader chooses. The excitement of the crowd lining the river-banks is very great, and the whole scene is as lively and picturesque a regatta as any river in the world can provide.

The time for the election of magistrates was altered from May to January 1st, the poll closing on the 31st of December previously.

1810.
Lieut.-Col.
J. Nugent
Smyth,
Supt.

The year 1812 is memorable for the erection of the first Protestant church in Central America. In that year Colonel Smyth laid the foundation-stone of the Protestant episcopal church of St. John the Baptist, on the site of the old barracks at Yarborough, the southern end of the town of Belize. It still remains; a neat, plain, brick erection, with a square tower (or rather now the stump of a tower).

1811-12.
Colonel
Smyth,
Superin-
tendent.

As far back as 1786, the chaplain of the united settlement of British Honduras and the Mosquito Shore had drawn attention to the subject of the ecclesiastical, and also the judicial establishments. But, as we have seen, that period was one of rapidly-occurring events, and the Rev. Mr. Shaw's plans were in abeyance until 1810, when it was decided in solemn assembly, that the Protestant religion known under the form and designation of the Church of England should be the dominant religion of the settlement, and an endowment was vested for the support of a clergyman, and the church to be erected.[3] The superintendent gave a grant of land

[3] Almanacs.

and the advowson (an advowson donative with cure of souls—incumbency by presentation, institution or induction) vested in the gift of the magistrates for the time being; churchwardens being appointed by the public meeting which resolved itself into a vestry annually for the purpose. The church thus established was included in the diocese of Jamaica. The endowment was 400*l.* per annum—300*l.* for the priest's stipend, 100*l.* for a clerk.

1813.　It is singular that this pious work was hardly completed when, next year, another terrible hurricane visited the settlement.

1814.　Government House was built on its present site close to St. John's church. Although frequently repaired, it is still an existing evidence of the durability of the timbers of the country in its posts and uprights.

The old treaties between England and Spain were renewed, and the conditions bearing reference to Honduras remained unaltered. The Spaniards, however, never made any further claim to the territory, and trade had sprung up between British and Spanish colonists, convenient to both and enriching the Belize traders, so that they by-and-by began to vie with the mahogany merchants in the race for wealth.

1815-16.
Colonel
Arthur,
superin-
endent.

Education next received attention, and a free school was founded in 1816. In the same year a king of the Mosquito Coast was crowned with much ceremony of the semi-ludicrous order at Belize. A recurrence of a similar investiture will receive more detailed description. A bridge across the River Belize was begun at Belize this year.

1817.　It would appear that this is the year in which the

crown first made grants of land on a proper system of record. Grants had previously been made after 1798.

The landing of some revolted negroes from Barbados was opposed by the inhabitants. The raising of the Prince Regent's Royal Regiment of Militia belongs to this year.

A new court-house was erected in 1819, and a 1818-19. criminal court established by imperial Act of Parliament. The superintendent was also now appointed under royal letters patent; so that the settlement assumed the recognized status of a colonial dependency attached to Jamaica.

Eboe Town, a section of the town of Belize reserved for that African tribe, was destroyed by fire.

The new bridge at Belize across the river was completed and opened for traffic.

Commodore Aury's independent squadron, says the Almanac, anchored off the Triangles, a group of islands a few miles south of Belize, after attacking and plundering Yzabal. The following year he treated Trujillo and Omoa in the same fashion. The commodore carried letters of marque, but was nothing else but a French pirate of the Paul Jones type, confining his depredations to Spanish property. A public hos- 1820-21. pital was instituted in 1820, and in 1821 a lighthouse was erected on Half-Moon Caye.

Meanwhile a great change had been steadily pro- 1821-23. gressing to its legitimate issue in the neighbouring Spanish countries of Mexico and Central America.

Guatemala took the initiative of giving effect to the liberal ideas spreading amongst these populations, originally most likely from the United States. On the

.15th September, 1821, at the palace of the Audencia, the independence of the state was proclaimed.

Iturbide, emperor of Mexico, which country had already thrown off allegiance to Spain, but preserved the monarchical form of government, succeeded in defeating the liberals of Guatemala, and the supremacy of the ephemeral emperor was declared, on the 5th of January, 1822, over the whole of New Spain.

But Iturbide's fall was not long delayed, and the five intendencias of Guatemala, San Salvador, Honduras, Nicaragua, and Costa Rica, agreed together to adopt the system of government of the United States of America, and formed a federal republic, based on popular representation and independent state organization.

Martial Law.

The superintendent, Colonel Arthur, who was also military commandant, seems to have involved himself in some unpleasantness with his military subordinates, and Major de la Houssaye and the other officers of the 2nd West India Regiment refused to obey orders. Martial law was proclaimed and existed from December 19th, 1821, to January 16th, 1822.

Major-Gen. Pye, Supt.

Discontent must have spread to the civilians, as we find a record of a memorial against Colonel Arthur, who was recalled this year (1822), and succeeded by Major-General Pye. Colonel Arthur's subsequent statements against the settlers, drew from them a reply dated 1823.

1823. Mosquitia.

The Mosquito Shore evacuated in compliance with the stipulations of the treaty of 1773, the British Government still remained anxious to preserve its influence in that quarter for reasons of its own.

Since the evacuation, therefore, the most friendly relations had been maintained with the half-civilized tribes inhabiting it. Captain Henderson, whose account of Honduras has more than once been referred to, paid the Shore an official visit during his term of service in this part of the world. He was sent in the schooner *Huntress,* in 1804, to convey a variety of presents ordered by the government for the chiefs of the Mosquito nation. He describes the Waiknas as a docile, but debased race, much given to donning cast-off uniforms, preferring, however, the upper garments and discarding the continuations. The chiefs and nobles were flattered by us, the kings successively pensioned and provided with a kind of keeper or guardian, euphemistically called a private secretary.

Blewfields, the capital of Mosquitia, is built on a river and lagoon of the same name. Baron Bulow, in furnishing to the London *Pictorial Times,* 1847, an account of a Prussian settlement near it, describes the situation as "beautiful." In it were the residence of the king (then named George II.) and of his secretary, Patrick Walker, Esq.; over the latter floated the royal standard of England. Notwithstanding repeated attempts, the Spaniards never succeeded in subjugating the territory. In 1820 Sir George McGregor was created cacique of Poyais by royal deed at the court of Cape Gracias á Dios : upon the strength of this he claimed absolute control of that part of the kingdom. One result of this was a project to found an English settlement on the Rio Tinto or Black River of the Poyais.

The scheme was most ridiculously managed, and

the bubble soon burst. The scattered remnants of its
dupes, military armament, theatrical company and all,
were to be discovered in exile about the Bay thirty
years after.

In 1823 the most helpless of the victims were removed to Belize, and the Baymen received the royal
approval of their humane conduct in coming to the
rescue of their unfortunate and misled fellow-country-
men. About 250 souls perished in the attempt to
colonize.

1824-25.   The coronation of King Robert of Mosquito,
took place at Belize on the 23rd of April, 1825.
King Robert, whom Henderson saw as a youth, had
been educated at Jamaica. His father was assassi-
nated by Prince Stephen, his intriguing brother.
Previous to the coronation ceremony, the rite of
baptism was administered to several of the chiefs
(caciques), they taking the names of celebrated individuals, as Lord Rodney, Lord Nelson, from the font.
The coronation was followed by a repast, at which the
newly-baptized and regenerate heathen nobility got
royally drunk. Dunn, in his History of Guatemala,
thus describes the scene:—" The smutty chiefs were
all ranged in state at the court-house, and had
undergone a complete metamorphosis; they were now
attired in cast-off coats of artillery and infantry officers,
and their appearance was anything but imposing.
The king, accompanied by British officers, went to
fetch the general (Major-General Codd, his Majesty's
superintendent), who returned with them and joined
the procession, as follows: public officers (civil)—
mounted officers of the garrison—general—the priest

—the *king*, with General Codd on his right, Major Nicholls on his left—the crown—merchants and inhabitants of Belize."

A commission to inquire into the mode of legal procedure of the settlement, arrived this year in H.M.S. *Valorous*, Captain the Earl of Huntingdon. The first printing establishment was set up, and a society for the promotion of Christian knowledge established. A road for cattle to the Haulover was cut.

This year is noticeable for the first visit of the bishop of the diocese. Bishop Lipscombe consecrated the church of St. John, and also held a confirmation service. 1826.

In this year Canning uttered his celebrated boast, "I called into existence the kingdoms of the New World to redress the balance of the Old!" Great Britain recognized the republics of Central and South America.

St. George's Caye submerged by a tidal wave during a hurricane. The Rev. Mr. Newport arrived as settlement-chaplain. 1827-28.

The garrison of Belize seized Ruatan. H.M.S. *Rangoon* and cutter *Chatham* surveyed the coast by order of the admiralty. 1829. Major A. McDonald, Acting Supt.

Hitherto there had been no trouble between the executive and legislative bodies, but during the acting commission of Major Alexander McDonald and that of his successor *en permanence*, Colonel Francis Cockburn, the accord was not maintained.

The public meeting (now beginning to call itself the legislative assembly), was undoubtedly a mere " creature of usage," as it has been called by a secretary of state (despatch to the Governor of Jamaica by the Secretary of State for Colonies, Downing Street, 30th December, 1842), but from time immemorial it had assumed legislative functions—"from the earlier days when the settlers, being under no regular government, took the opportunity of their assembling together on the coast, for the purpose of shipping their mahogany and logwood, to make regulations for the well-being of their community."[4] And this assumption of legislative power, as well as the investiture of the annually-elected magistrates with judicial functions, and the control of the finances, had been tolerated by successive secretaries of state and the superintendents appointed as yet. Interference with these rights now irritated the settlers. But the state of political feeling does not appear to have affected the prosperity of the settlement:—

Year.	Revenue.		Expenditure.
	£		£
1824	14,346		8,486
1825	16,000	(round	10,580
1826	16,000	figures)	8,253
1827	16,825		24,830
1828	16,000	(round	16,275
1829	16,000	figures)	16,473

[4] Memorandum to the Earl of Aberdeen, Secretary of State for the Colonies, from Colonel Cockburn, 1835.

SHIPMENTS OF WOOD, ETC.

1824, Mahogany	.	5,500,000 feet.
1825, ,,	.	5,783,590 ,,
1826, ,,	.	6,379,000 ,,
1827, ,,	.	7,743,486 ,,
,, Cedar .	.	15,643 ,,
,, Logwood	.	1,856 tons.
,, Tortoise-shell.		1,386 lbs.
,, Sarsaparilla .		19,753 ,,
,, Indigo .	.	183,960 ,,
,, Cochineal	.	63,551 ,,

(Duty on mahogany, £3 16s. per ton.)

1825, Cedar .	.	2,196 tons.
,, Logwood	.	4,825 ,,
,, Tortoise-shell.		3,915 lbs.

From London Prices Current.

Average price, Mahogany, 18*l.* per M. feet.
   ,,   ,,   Logwood, 6*l.* to 6*l.* 5*s.* per ton.
   ,,   ,,   Tortoise-shell, 1*l.* 19*s.* to 2*l.* 2*s.* per lb.
   ,,   ,,   Sarsaparilla, 2*s.* 6*d.* to 3*s.* per lb.
   ,,   ,,   Indigo, 3*s.* to 5*s.* per lb.
   ,,   ,,   Cochineal, 12*s.* 6*d.* to 14*s.* per lb.

Vessels, 1st July to 31st December, 1827.

British 25, French 1—26 Inwards, 6496 tons.
  ,, 40,   ,,   1—41 Outwards 10,731 tons.

The population in 1826 was 5,197. In 1829, 3,833. Falling off unexplained.

To the above returns of trade must be superadded the transit trade of transient traders who paid a tax, the trade with North America, and that with the new republics, which had sprung up since the substitution of an *ad valorem* duty of five per cent. on the abolition of the old prohibitory one of thirty-three per cent. on foreign goods imposed by the jealous commercial policy of old Spain.

CHAPTER VIII.

CROWN *v.* COLONY, 1830-42.

1830-39.   THE crown had now begun to adopt quite a different policy with regard to the settlers and their institutions. King Log had come at last.

1835.   In 1835, Colonel Cockburn directed Mr. Thomas Miller, the keeper of the records, to draw up a memorandum showing the difficulties the superintendent had to deal with in his administration of the affairs of the settlement, judicial, financial, and economical. The memorandum, after a by no means accurate topographical description, and account of the trade, products, inhabitants, &c., enters at length upon the question of the tenure of the soil, advocating negotiations being opened with Spain for a full cession of the territory before the neighbouring republics put in claims. The memorandum was addressed to the Earl of Aberdeen, then at the head of the Colonial Office, who wisely did not adopt the suggestion, but was satisfied with the *de facto* possession, allowing, as lawyers would say, the other side to commence an action for ejectment. The subject was, however, mooted by our minister at Madrid, during the negotiations for a definite treaty between Mexico and Spain, in 1835-36. Some such

attempt had been made by the central government of
the federation in a late grant to a Colonel Galindo, of
land actually in possession of the British, but nothing
came of it. The document then proceeds to describe
the constitution. The public meeting assembles (the
memorandum says) of its own accord once every four
months. To this body a 400*l. currency* qualification is
necessary, but limited to British-born subjects; a can-
didate for election must be proposed by a member and
returned by twenty-six votes, and was elected for life.
The voters' qualifications to vote being the same as the
candidates to sit as members, except that the property
qualification is only 100*l. currency,* and two years'
residence. The body has no limit to its numbers; it
then consisted of sixty-five members. It is not called
together by the superintendent, and there was no
authority for its existence from the crown, but it
originated in the early customs of the settlers themselves. (This is correct; but a settlement which had
been left for 200 years—from its origin—to govern
itself had certainly acquired the right of legislating for
itself through its representatives in public assembly.)
The memorandum then bluntly states : " This meeting
until the last ten years could confer upon the discussion of any question that a member thought fit to
propose, but a check has been put to the exercise of
the privilege by a late regulation of the superintendent, which requires all notices of motion to be submitted to him for approval, and to be advertised for a
certain period, previous to being brought forward at
the meeting." The proceedings of the meeting in
electing the chairman and addressing the superinten-

dent by deputation—his message in return discussed and replied to—motions next discussed and formed into laws of the settlement or rejected—supplies granted for the ensuing four months—and, the meeting having resolved itself into a vestry and elected churchwardens, dissolving, are then detailed in the memorandum. The proceedings are transmitted to the superintendent who has the power of veto. The annual election of, magistrates at one of the yearly meetings is then described, and the financial powers granted them. " They usually report their proceedings to the superintendent, who, in the event of any misapplication of the public money, would, it is believed, take upon himself to interfere."

" The magisterial body, until the last two years, was appointed by vote of the inhabitants, and went out of office every year. They are now appointed by the superintendent for the same period. In addition to this anomalous legislature, it is to be remarked that the magistrates have been in the habit of making laws by themselves alone." [No instances of this are given.] " The superintendent also legislates by proclamation on occasions when he may consider it necessary."

It was this very matter of proclamations, and the interference, above-stated by the memorandum, with the power to originate and discuss independent motions, of which the inhabitants complained. Two memorials had already been forwarded by them, one, in 1831, to Lord Stanley (the late Earl of Derby), the other to Spring Rice, Esq. (afterwards Lord Monteagle), and the Duke of Wellington, in 1834, detailing their grievances, and asking for the lands to be given the settlers, and that the imports from the settlement into England, should be put on the same footing as those from other West Indian colonies. The memorandum of Colonel Cockburn was obviously a counterblast. " Colonel Cockburn," it continues, " has received the assurance of Sir George Murray, Mr. Secretary Stanley, and Mr. Secretary Rice, that it is the intention of his Majesty's government to take an early opportunity of remodelling the legislative institutions of Honduras ;" and it is recommended " to abolish the public meeting altogether," and substitute for it " a council of *advice,* to consist of six persons "—but if that suggestion be not adopted, it is not recommended to attempt its improvement except by withdrawing from it the power of assembling and dissolving without the authority of the superintendent.

The memorandum next diverges to the difficulties in the administration of justice, its views on which will be referred to hereafter. Finances are alluded to ; " the public debt on the 30th September last amounting to 7500*l.*," and a paper currency having been issued which " had on the face of it a mere obligation on the part of the public of Honduras to pay interest on its value, at the rate of six per cent." until redeemed. " It is not a legal tender," and is stated to have then been commonly discounted at from ten to fifteen per cent. The superintendent complains that his efforts to have it made legal tender were opposed by the assembly. He recommends the soil being given to the settlers for cultivation, in compliance with the memorials, and grants of land being made to them.

Occupiers of town-lots, banks, and plantations, were to be confirmed in their holdings in perpetuity; but former grants or permissions of extensive lands for cutting wood were not to be considered as giving present occupiers permanent possession, but merely priority of claim to a new grant.

The memorandum concludes by pointing out the difficulties in reference to transient foreign traders, the impolicy of the American tonnage-duty, and difficulty in registration of vessels. He applies for a small vessel of war to be stationed permanently at Belize, and recommends that, if any steps be taken to open fresh negotiations with Spain and the Spanish republics on the subject of territorial title, Ruatan and Bonaca ought to be included in the British claims to possession, as, from their contiguity, they ought not to be in the hands of a hostile power or a commercial rival. The memorandum, evidently drawn up in reply to the memorials of 1833-34 from the inhabitants, is right on many points, and shows how much on legislative, financial, and judicial questions Colonel Cockburn was at variance with the people he was sent out to rule. Another memorial from the inhabitants, similar in substance to those of 1833-34, more submissive in tone, was forwarded in 1839, but was left also without reply.

1834. On the 1st of August, 1834, the emancipation of the negroes in the British West Indies was consummated.

Total abolition did not take place simultaneously in Honduras. A more gradual process of manumission was wisely adopted. The slave-owners of Honduras did not, of course, share in the compensation allowed

other possessors of slaves who manumitted in 1834; but
they curtailed voluntarily by two years the continu-
ance of the intermediate system known as the appren-
ticeship of predial labourers. No excesses or diminution of labour resulted from abolition. It took place
on the 1st of August, 1838, although not due by the
arrangements with the home government until two
years after.

The resumption of the post of superintendent
by Colonel Alexander McDonald at this time, did not
allay the irritation caused by recent alterations in the
constitution of the settlement, and encroachments on
ancient rights and customs. *1837. Col. A. McDonald, Supt.*

The colonel was a fine, tall Highlander—a soldier
of the Peninsula—and perhaps just a little too deeply
imbued with the martinet spirit then dominant in
military circles, to make a judicious or popular civil
governor.

Beyond exercising the veto on disbursements, he
controlled the finances by interfering with the right
of the assembly to vote supplies, denying the public
meetings power to debate any motion until he had
approved of it. Hitherto, the control of the disbursements had been in the hands of the magistrates, who
were accountable to the public meeting alone, that
legislative body voting all sums for expenditure. And
it was subsequently laid down by a secretary of
state's despatch, that "all grants must be made to
the crown, and the expenditure of them must be
committed to the executive authority. But on the
other hand the executive authority ought to govern
itself by the terms of the appropriation, and if grants

aré made which are objectionable, either as to their appropriation or as to the conditions attached to them, the superintendent should decline to sanction such grants, and he ought not to accept the money and violate the conditions."[1]

But Colonel McDonald gave more cause for complaint by his arbitrary measures and his legislating by proclamation. In one of these autocratic missives he goes the length of assuming the right of "confining in the common gaol any individual acting against his authority or obstructing his mandate."

1840. In this year the ancient usages and customs were finally abrogated as far as the administration of justice was concerned, and it was proclaimed that "the law of England is and shall be the law of this settlement or *colony* of British Honduras." Old Burnaby was knocked on the head. The superintendent also appointed an executive council to assist him in the administration of affairs.

During the period now under retrospect the trade with the interior steadily increased. From 119,000*l.* currency in 1824, it was estimated to have risen this year to 300,000*l.* currency. It began to be of importance also with the peninsula of Yucatan, transient traders arriving from Campeché and Sisal to make purchases.

Peace in the neighbouring new-born republics continued up to 1838 unbroken. The following is a statement of the revenue and expenditure for the ten years:—

[1] Secretary of state's despatch, quoted by Colonel McDonald himself, in his letter to chairman of public meeting, 31st October, 1842, in *Observer*, No. 50, vol. ii., 3rd November, 1842.

	Revenue.			Expenditure.		
	£	s.	d.	£	s.	d.
1830 . . .	14,931	11	6	13,278	6	2
1831 . . .	11,712	8	11	11,525	15	0
1832 . . .	14,050	5	11	16,997	18	10
1833 . . .	12,732	2	5	14,113	15	8
1834 . . .	14,706	0	0	14,241	10	2
1835 . . .	16,860	3	3	13,915	9	2
1836 . . .	17,799	14	1	12,771	17	8
1837 . . .	13,945	12	3	13,770	5	5
1838 . . .	15,739	7	2	16,592	16	4
1839 . . .	13,752	15	4	15,970	15	1
1840 . . .	12,246	5	3	12,537	8	5

In 1830-31 the export of mahogany fell two and a half millions of feet, having retrograded since 1826-27, in consequence of overtrading and a glut in the home market. It began to increase again to three, four, five, six millions of feet each successive year, until 1837, when it reached eight and a half millions. This 1837 was a particularly prosperous year. Other articles increased also in the amount exported.

The following statement for the six months, from 1840-41. October 1st, 1840, to September 30th, 1841, may be compared with any previous twelve months, for which statistics have already been given :—

Cedar	12,248 feet
Logwood	5546 tons
Fustic	33¼ tons
Rosewood	118 pieces
Cochineal	6201 seroons
Indigo	1746 ,,
Sarsaparilla	106,734 lbs.
Cocoa-nuts	129,400
Tortoise-shell	880 lbs.

9233 logs mahogany, 4,571,056 feet.
600 lbs. cotton, 3068 ox-hides, and 24 bags rice.[2]

[2] From true copy of statement from government secretary's office

The new articles on the list show that attempts were thus early being made to introduce new staples of export. The total imports for the period were in value 382,915*l.* 19*s.* 6*d.*; tonnage :—vessels, 112; tons, 21,862. The total value of exports, 400,000*l.* A specimen of home-grown tobacco was exhibited this year.

The population was considerably reduced at this time.

The statement shows a fair amount of business for so small a community, but in the principal staple production of the country, mahogany, there had been a great deterioration in price within the last few years, while there had been greatly increased public expenditure, and consequent burdens on the inhabitants and their commerce. Belize was not without its Joseph Humes to advocate retrenchment and accuse the executive of extravagance. Following the abolition of slavery, slave-grown sugar was placed at a differential duty of double that levied on free-grown, viz. 20*s.* per ton.

1841. It will perhaps be as well to let the inhabitants now speak for themselves. Their memorials to the home government not meeting with any response they this year drew up two fresh petitions. A fair idea of the state of the settlement will be obtained from the following extracts :—

" The petition[3] of the members of the legislative assembly of Belize, Honduras, humbly showeth :—

" That your petitioners are British-born subjects, settled and established on this coast, industriously occupied as mahogany-cutters and merchants.

*   *   *   *   *

[3] *Honduras Observer*, No. 16, vol. i., March 10, 1841.

" That within the last half-century Belize consisted
of a few wretched huts, in the midst of a miserable
swamp; but the spirit and perseverance of the inhabitants have, with scarcely more aid than the mere
countenance of the mother-country, elevated the
settlement of Belize into an important appendage of
the British empire, changed the huts of fifty years
since into well-built houses, and from a miserable
swamp have raised a town flourishing in its commerce,
giving employment annually to 20,000 tons of British
shipping, and increased its imports to nearly half a
million sterling of British manufacture.

*   *   *   *   *

" That the inhabitants of Belize have long retained
and flourished under a primitive state of government,
left by the mother-country almost wholly to their own
views of internal policy, and almost to their own resources for its support and expenditure.

" That thus left to themselves the loyalty of the inhabitants has never been impugned (fondly clinging
to their constitution as the palladium of their rights,
and their shield from oppression), and in the late
anxious change in the state of their labouring population, your petitioners went cheerfully, voluntarily, and
without prompting, hand and hand with the views of
the parent government. . . Neither diminution of
labour or the fruits of labour, nor increase of crime,
has obtained from the total abolition of slavery in the
settlement.

" That your petitioners humbly pray reference may
be had to the report of the commissioners of legal
inquiry of the years 1825 and 1826, wherein the pro-

cess of the judicial courts of this settlement is highly approved of, and that no appeal has ever been made from their courts of justice to any higher tribunal."

[The petition then goes on to point out the mode of election of magistrates, their control of finance and judicature vested in them by the public assembly, and proceeds :—]

"That, within the last two years, her Majesty's superintendent, Colonel Alexander McDonald, C.B., has on various occasions legislated by proclamation, by which the acts of this legislative assembly have been rendered a nullity. Not, your petitioners would respectfully observe, by a constitutional exercise of the acts by the superintendent, but he wholly and entirely superseding our authority, and assuming to himself the legislative, judicial, and executive power."

[The proclamation of the superintendent with reference to confining individuals in the common gaol, is then "viewed with dismay," &c.; his assertion in his messages to the assembly, 4th and 5th March, 1839, "of full and entire control over the revenue," is repudiated, and the proclamation of the laws of England as the future laws of the settlement is "viewed with astonishment, inasmuch as the laws of England have always been in force, except in some few cases where the constitution of society and circumstances purely local rendered a deviation from them unavoidable."

The petition closes with the following demands :—]

" Your petitioners therefore pray they may be allowed freedom of discussion in their public deliberations . . . the right of enacting local laws for their internal government and guidance . . . and for the right of raising a revenue from their own resources, and of applying the same to the contingencies and support of their institutions and government."

This petition is signed by a committee of four, and dated the 2nd of March, 1841. The second opens thus :—

" That your petitioners are British subjects, settled under a superintendent appointed by the crown, in that part of the Bay of Honduras known as British Yucatan. [This is the only occasion met with of its being so called in the progress of extended researches.] That the trade of the settlers having been hitherto confined to the cutting of mahogany and logwood, until the recent independence of the Spanish American republics has of late years opened to them a market for British goods to the extent of half a million sterling, and the cutting of the said woods having become a very precarious employment, your petitioners are desirous of acquiring the unquestionable right of cultivating this extensive soil, with a *bonâ fide* title of property in the arable lands thereof [a mistake, it may be said, to raise this question of title], and with unrestricted permission to export such cultivated products from this, and to have them imported into the United Kingdom at the same rate of duties as from the British West India Islands."

[The petitioners then refer to their former memorials.]

" No climate or soil can be better adapted for the productions of the tropics than those of British Honduras. In particular, lands near the sea can, by free labour, furnish every variety of cotton, and those bordering on the lagoons could grow abundance of rice and tobacco."

After statistics in reference to the production of these articles in the United States, and their exportation to Great Britain, the memorialists dwell on the fall in value of mahogany, which sold in 1835-36 at a price equal to 18*l.* and 20*l.* sterling, and now " will not bring more on the spot than 9*l.* to 12*l.* per 1000 feet." The petitioners conclude by reiterating their requests for possession of the soil for cultivation, the right to cultivate and to export on the same terms as the West India Islands.

Until a reply was received, the assembly determined to transact no public business. The superintendent continued to carry on the government by proclamation and with the aid of the executive council.

During a visit this year to the Mosquito Shore, in H.M.S. *Tweed,* accompanied by his private secretary, Patrick Walker, Esq., Colonel McDonald executed some very high-handed proceedings towards the State of Nicaragua, which had a boundary dispute with the Mosquitoes near Cape Gracias. He actually landed and made Colonel Quijano, Comandante of San Juan del Norte, prisoner, removing him on board the *Tweed.* Of course this led to a warm correspondence. Five British merchants were imprisoned as a reprisal by the Central American authorities.

It was notified that the affairs of the colony were under consideration by Mr. Labouchere and the Board of Trade. Colonel McDonald this year proceeded with a few officers to, and hoisted the British flag on, the island of Ruatan.

The year 1842 begins with a second visitation by the diocesan, when it was mooted to have a second clergyman for the settlement, and to build a chapel of ease to St. John's church.

Public officials were, by an act passed this year, in future, to be paid by salaries instead of by fees, and a committee managed the new scale of salaries and the altered schedule of fees. H.M. superintendent's salary was fixed at 3000*l.* currency; clerk of courts, 1000*l.*; public treasurer, 1000*l.*; queen's advocate, 1000*l.*, with private practice; rector, 1000*l.*; colonial secretary, 1000*l.*; provost marshal, 833*l.*, and others in proportion.

About June, the chairman of the public meeting, W. H. Coffin, Esq., received a reply to the memorial of 1841, from Sir C. Metcalf, the enlightened Governor of Jamaica, the contents of his despatch being directed to be published to the meeting.

" The public meeting is authorized by her Majesty's Government to continue to exercise its legislative powers, harmoniously if it can, with the executive, each taking usage as the rule by which their respective powers are to be defined." And in a subsequent despatch it is intimated that her Majesty's Government has " not yet determined on what principles the future constitution of the settlement shall be based." Sir Charles also lays down the principle " that it is in the nature of popular assemblies to check the excessive power by the executive government, and that the free constitution of Great Britain has arisen from proceedings animated by this spirit." Colonel McDonald took the admonition in good part, and in his communications to the meeting became quite conciliatory, alleging the late differences to have arisen from "that sole cause, that we claimed severally the exercise of functions each of us considered we had a title to maintain," and solemnly delegates to it all legislative duties.

But there was still a question at issue between the executive and the legislative—the control of the finances. Since 1833 the magistrates were no longer the elected of the people, but the nominees of the crown, i.e. the superintendent. Were they then to retain the control of the expenditure of the sums voted by the assembly? The assembly contended not, but urged that, "under the altered circumstances of the appointment of the magistracy, the meeting should adopt measures to ensure the proper and economical appropriation of the public funds." They did not propose to take the control away from the magistrates, but placed them as usual at their disposal under certain conditions and restrictions, and in doing so they were, it must be granted, acting constitutionally.

In former years the qualifications for the magistracy were three years' residence and the possession of 500*l.* visible "property." Then they had unlimited control of expenditure, the assembly voting the supplies. In 1829 Colonel McDonald himself asked the meeting to curtail these powers of the bench, alleging extravagant dealings with the public moneys against them.

The question of judicial reform also arose. It had been suggested by Colonel McDonald that a chief justice should be appointed at a salary of 1000*l.* a year. Lord Stanley intimates to Sir C. Metcalf, March 31st, 1842, that, if the public meeting gave the superintendent the authority to create the office and votes the salary, he " does not anticipate any difficulty in finding a competent person to fill it."

" The difficulties in the administration of justice," according to Colonel Cockburn's memorandum, "arise principally from the limited jurisdiction of the supreme court of criminal judicature, the only court in the settlement which is founded on a legal basis." It was created in 1821 under the great seal, and took cognizance only of five crimes—murder, manslaughter, rape, robberies, and burglaries [query arsons ?]. The superintendent presided with the two judges on the bench. The grand court took cognizance of the minor crimes, and sat for the trial of suits and actions at law, and there were, besides, the summary court and the police court, presided over by the sitting magistrates.

The head of the executive presiding on the bench was certainly an anomalous arrangement. This year an act passed for the appointment of a legal judge, and henceforward the executive and judicial functions were kept distinct.

There were great complaints at this time of depression in trade. Mahogany exportation fell to 4,500,000 feet. The total value of exports for the six months to September 30th was 322,140*l.* sterling; imports, 193,656*l.* (including 32,946*l.* from the United States) : showing, as compared with the previous twelve months a falling off in imports of more than half, 195,259*l.*, exports, 63,189*l.* sterling.

The falling off in imports is attributed to excessive importation in the two or three years preceding. The states of Central America were very much disturbed, which interfered with the transit trade of the colony. The war between the "Liberales," under Morazan, against the "Serviles," or clerical and reactionary party, had assumed a new phase by the accession to the latter of Carrera and his hordes of Indian mountaineers. Morazan, a native of Spanish Honduras, was an amiable and attractive leader and an enlightened patriot, the son of a French creole. For fifteen years he was the mainstay of the liberals of Central America, he preserved tranquillity tolerably well up to 1838, but the half-breed Carrera coming to the aid of the "Serviles," and Malespin revolting in San Salvador, Morazan was unable to make head against both. He carried on the struggle till 1842. In September of that year he was finally defeated by Carrera, taken prisoner, and, as a matter of course, shot.

CHAPTER IX.

1842 to 1850.

CONTINUATION OF THE STRUGGLE BETWEEN THE EXECUTIVE AND PUBLIC MEETING.

A CHANGE now took place in the sentiments and line 1843. of conduct of the bench of magistrates. They were no longer, as they had been by usage, chosen from the members of the assembly, and now asserted independence of, even superiority to, that body, considering themselves part of the executive; especially they pursued an independent course of action in controlling the disbursements of the sums voted for public expenditure by the public meeting. In this they were supported by the superintendent.

In placing restrictions on the expenditure of certain votes—contingency votes for example—the public meeting may have acted constitutionally; but the superintendent and the magistracy had right on their side in denying the public meeting the power to interfere with the control of expenditure of sums they had once for all placed at the disposal of the executive. Colonel Cockburn was right in saying that in case of misappropriation by the magistrates the superintendent would most probably interfere. Such was his duty; on the other hand, the Secretary of State's despatch already quoted in the preceding chapter lays down the course to be pursued in regard to the appropriation of grants by the public meeting; this despatch was communicated to the meeting by Colonel McDonald, in his message of 31st October, 1842.

By the packet of June 15th, his Excellency Colonel Charles St. John Fancourt arrived to relieve Colonel McDonald, and with him came Robert Temple, Esq., barrister-at-law, to assume the duties of the newly-created office of chief justice.

Colonel Fancourt struck the key-note of the policy he intended should mark his administration in the first message he sent to the meeting. "I am instructed to impress upon you, that the public meeting at Honduras has no right, strictly speaking, to legislate, though it may with the consent of the superintendent make rule for the conduct of the settlement."

The public meeting had been the "creature of usage," it was now to be made the creature of the executive. Similar instructions, it has been evident, had been issued to Colonel Fancourt's two immediate predecessors to initiate and pursue the same line of policy. That policy was skilfully to withdraw from the public meeting its constitutional powers and privileges, and to subvert the influence of the people in the government. The suspension of the free election annually of the seven magistrates and their nomination in future by the crown, was a deadly blow to the constitution; the withdrawal of the power to originate motions and freely discuss them was the second; the gradual increase in the exercise of the veto by the superintendent, and separation of the magisterial body from a common interest with the public meeting, further continued the same machiavelian policy. Small as Honduras is, a political student may gain a hint or two from studying its history.

But Colonel Fancourt was a diplomatist by training, and a courtier, and knew well how to conceal the iron hand of arbitrary authority under the silken glove of a bland and courteous manner. Matters progressed favourably for a time.

"We take pleasure," says the *Honduras Observer* of the 18th May, 1843, in announcing that the first "steamer built in this settlement was launched on Saturday, and named the *British Honduras.*" She was built by Messrs. Grant and Munro, to ply about the Cayes. We read no more about her in the papers.

The two principal courts of the settlement were now 1843-46. precisely the same in their constitution, both being presided over by the chief justice, with two puisne or assistant-judges sitting with him, the supreme court having the same jurisdiction as formerly, the grand court taking cognizance of minor crimes, and acting as a court of oyer and terminer in civil actions. The summary and police courts were left to magisterial superintendence. In 1845 the public meeting defined and limited the powers of the chief justice, the judges and the several courts. The grand court could imprison for four years, or fine up to 500*l.* currency. The summary court required three or more justices on the bench, and had power to imprison for three months, or fine up to 50*l.* currency. An attempt to introduce regular legal practitioners into the courts, originating with the chief justice, was again and again successfully resisted.

Chief Justice Temple was a sound lawyer, and a man of ability, but arbitrary, dogmatical, and in his personal antipathies vindictive. In place of tentatively and gradually introducing legal reforms, he attempted so to do *vi et armis,* and naturally roused opposition; he soon became extremely unpopular, and his unpopularity continued, and even increased, during his occupancy of the high post he held in the settlement.

Trade was affected by the disturbances beyond the frontiers during the whole of this period; the duty on mahogany was raised fifteen per cent. by the United States, from December 1st, 1846, but the simultaneous presence of seven vessels of that nationality in the harbour was hailed as an augury of future trade with that country which has proved a correct one.

> 1845. Revenue, 22,372*l.*   Expenditure, 18,302*l.*
> 1846.   „   21,667*l.*   „   19,200*l.*
> 1846. Exports, 408,188*l.*
>   „   Imports, 243,725*l.*
> Mahogany shipped, 1845, 9,319,507 feet.
>   „   „   1846, 13,719,075 feet.
> (Some portion cut beyond the limits.)
> Number of vessels, 152.   Tonnage, 39,485 tons.

1847-48. The year 1847 proved itself one of considerable internal excitement and dissension.

1847. Revenue   27,798*l.*
 „   Expenditure 36,348*l.*
 ───────────
Difference   8550*l.*

An act was passed for abolishing the unpaid magistracy and substituting a stipendiary police-magistrate and justice of the peace. The assistant-judges were to be appointed under the seal of the colony. Also acts relative to Dissenters, for establishing the office of attorney-general, for the maintenance of good order in the community, and for the registration of foreign residents. This latter act was rendered necessary by one result of the outbreak of the "guerra de castas" in Yucatan, which drove bodies of Yucatecan Spaniards as refugees across the northern frontier into our territory. Great alarm prevailed throughout the settlement that the sheltering of these refugees would bring upon it Indian raids and reprisals. Both parties in the contest sought the British of Honduras as allies, and each watched closely our dealings with the other. The public meeting voted for defence a sum of 5000*l.* and, as usual, applied to Jamaica for reinforcements, which arrived, and troops were stationed on the Hondo under Lieutenant Glubb. The scare did not pass off until the Indians, having taken Salamanca-Bacalar, requested to be permitted to trade on the same terms as the Yucatecans had previously done.

At the capture of Bacalar, the Spanish colonists are said to have behaved with great cowardice, the Santa Cruz Indians to have exhibited great ferocity and committed many atrocities.

The Ladinos or Mestizos [1] of Yucatan (and there are but a very few families who can boast the pure "sangre azul" of old Spain in the western peninsula) are about one-fifth of the population, or about 500,000, and are much degenerated from the war-like conquerors of New Spain, speaking a miserable *patois.* Of the 400,000 Indians, some are peaceable, the majority untamed enemies of all rule.

1849.　Major O'Connor, commanding the troops on the Hondo, visited Bacalar in 1849 to mediate, and reported seeing roasted bodies. In May, the Spaniards retook Bacalar, to lose it again in July, when a Colonel Rosado was killed. He was commandant. The fort still held out for the Spaniards.

The differences between Great Britain and Nicaragua on account of the boundaries of the Mosquito kingdom, did not affect the settlement much. Mr. Patrick Walker, ex-private secretary to the late superintendent, Colonel McDonald, would appear to have been superseded as the keeper of the Mosquito king and his affairs by her Majesty's Consul-General for Central America, Fred. Chatfield, Esq., who undertook negotiations. We laid claim to the Roman River, and took San Juan del Norte, calling it Greytown, notwithstanding protests from Nicaragua and other republics making common cause with her. Tigre, a beautiful island in the Gulf of Fonseca, was at the same time ceded to the United States by Nicaragua. All this consular activity may be laid to a scheme for an inter-oceanic canal. In 1849, Commodore Paynter and Consul-General Chatfield seized the island of Tigre, lately

[1] The names given the mixed race sprung from Spanish and Indian blood in Central America.

ceded to the United States. The United States' Consul protested, but Mr. Chatfield would do no more than refer the question, retaining his conquest. So matters stood at the opening of 1850.

It is only to-day that the Emperor Francis Joseph of Austria has settled the disputes between Nicaragua and Great Britain by arbitration (1882).

The executive council of Honduras now consisted of the chief justice, attorney-general, colonial secretary, and public treasurer.

BELIZE PRICES CURRENT.

Flour $7 @ $8 per barrel.	Pork, Mess $19 @ 20 per barrel.		
Pilot Bread $7 ,, ,,	,, Prime $17 @ $18 ,, ,,
Navy ,, $6½ ,, ,,	Beef, Mess $16 ,, ,,
Indian Corn $2½ @ $3 ,,	,, Family $18 ,, ,,
	,, Prime $14 ,, ,,

"All at loggerheads," may be an expression beneath 1847-48. the dignity of even so humble a historical retrospect as the present. Nevertheless, it is the only one which can adequately convey the state of affairs in Honduras brought about by Chief Justice Temple. The legislative body was still recalcitrant and had its own subjects of dispute with the executive and the magistracy—such as the increase of expenditure—but Mr. Temple was soon at variance with the executive, the legislative and the judicial elements, and had roused the ire of the whole venire of jurors.

The first bubble of the "hot water," in which the settlement was kept for some few years, was a prosecution by the attorney-general for seditious libel, of the editor of the *Honduras Observer and Gazette*, Mr. Fitzgibbon—an alien, an American by birth, an Irishman by descent. The crown failed to obtain a verdict.

Mr. Temple next plunged into the hot bath over head and ears, by a wholesale aspersion of the jurymen of the settlement, in a letter to the superintendent, which Mr. Fitzgibbon somehow obtained and published. Three-fourths of the jury-list memorialized the superintendent, requesting to be exempted from being called upon to serve while Mr. Temple sat; this of course the superintendent could not grant, and at the next grand court, 28th April, 1848, some ten jurors refused to be empanelled. The jurymen were imprisoned, and at the same court Fitzgibbon was fined 100*l*. currency, and sentenced to six months' imprisonment, and whilst in gaol was very rigorously dealt with.

These were harsh and injudicious measures, but the judges were only carrying out the law. However foolish and wrong Mr. Temple's letter to the superintendent, it was a privileged communication, not meant for publication, and the editor was properly fined; his imprisonment might have been omitted.

The jurors on their part, by refusing their obvious duty, were not seeking redress of their unmistakable grievance in the proper way. The superintendent kept himself as much as possible out of the fracas. His conduct may be viewed in different lights, but it should be remembered he was involved in trouble with the assembly, having refused to compel the treasurer to produce certain vouchers at the assembly's request, while he himself was also embroiled with the fiery Temple. The act of 1845, passed by the assembly and sanctioned by him, defining the powers of the courts and judges, had displeased the head of the justiciary, and that functionary did not hesitate to address the Governor of Jamaica directly on the subject of his grievance. In his letter to Lord Elgin, March 18th, 1845, he professes to uphold "the authority of the courts of law of this settlement, and the independence of the judges," asserting that, " against that authority and that independence a fatal blow has been aimed by her Majesty's superintendent, and that small section of the inhabitants which constitute the public meeting." He also intimates that he will treat the act (above referred to) as " a nullity until it shall have received the sanction of her Majesty in council."

Lord Elgin's reply, dated 30th May, 1845, is diplomatic and unsatisfactory, pats the superintendent on the back, and indecisively and mildly admonishes the chief justice to be more respectful in his language when speaking of the public meeting. The correspondence was not published until April, 1848.[1]

The next person to fall under Mr. Temple's displeasure was a Mr. W. H. Coffin, one of the leading merchants, who had long taken the lead in public affairs, been almost perpetual chairman of the meeting by choice of the members, annually elected to the magistracy for years, and was then colonel of militia, and an assistant-judge. A motion of the meeting condemnatory of Mr. Temple's letter with reference to the jurors having been signed or joined in by Mr. Coffin, the chief justice complained to the superintendent, who rightly judging Mr. Coffin in error in so doing, being on the bench, deprived him of his judgeship.

The newspapers—the *Observer and Gazette,* in oppo-

[1] *Honduras Observer,* April 15, 1848.

sition to a new one, the *Central American Times,* started
for the purpose in support of the government—képt
the excitement up.

In viewing at this distance of time this general scrim-
mage between the executive, legislative, and judicial
bodies, one can only regret that there was not a states-
man of the capacity and firmness of Sir C. Metcalfe at
the head of affairs in Jamaica, to point out to the superintendent the limits of his authority, to recommend
reforms in the legislative chamber, and to curb the
pugnacious temper of the chief justice. Memorials
were addressed through the Governor of Jamaica, Sir
C. Grey, for administrative changes, and one for the
removal of Mr. Temple, without, however, succeeding
in producing any intervention on the part of the
Colonial Office.

| 1848. Expenditure £28,361 | 1849. Expenditure £27,610 |
| „ Revenue £20,361 | „ Revenue £20,979 |

Towards the close of 1848, a better feeling existed
between the superintendent and the public meeting,
but the unpopularity of Mr. Temple continued to increase. At the grand court of November, 1848, Mr.
Coffin was find 100*l.* currency, and sentenced to six
months' imprisonment for contempt of court, for refusing to answer whether he was or not the writer of
certain letters, signed " Young Belize," in the *Observer,*
reflecting on the chief justice. Mr. Coffin was not the
author (but a Mr. M. F. Sterling, who was discharged with an admonition) ; Mr. Coffin therefore
merely suffered for obstinacy, which many regarded as
noble firmness. The excitement caused by this was
very great, Mr. Coffin being extremely popular, and

on his release in the February following, by orders
from Sir Charles Grey, there were grand manifestations
of the people's sympathy and delight.

There was great depression in trade in 1848-49.

The depression of trade continued, and it is now
that the key-note was struck of the tune which has
been harped upon ever since—the decline of the
mahogany interest.

1850.

About this period a second church or chapel of ease
was finished and opened. The Baptist persuasion also
built their present meeting-house. Ecclesiastical
affairs were not exempt, however, from the prevailing
epidemic of dissension. Colonel Fancourt interfered
with the patronage of St. John's, and there were two
rival claimants for the rectory, the Rev. M. Newport
and the Rev. T. Coghlan.

Chief Justice Temple was thrashed in the streets by
young Coghlan, Mr. Temple having brought this youth
and another before the police-magistrate on a frivolous
charge of larceny. The attorney-general, Mr. Lewis,
resigned, and an unsuccessful movement was made
to abolish the office. The mails were now carried
between Jamaica and Belize by the Royal Mail
Steamer *Conway*. The superintendent made au
attempt at mediation between the contending races
in Yucatan, and visited the peninsula. His good
offices were not appreciated by either combatants.

An insurrection in Guatemala gained some advantage
over Carrera's forces.

CHAPTER X.

MAHOGANY AND TIMBER TRADE OF HONDURAS GENERALLY.

1850.   THE rise and progress of the British settlement whose
history we have imperfectly traced have been indis-
solubly connected with the fortunes of its trade in
timber and dye-woods.   When London and Liverpool
prices current showed an advance in the rates for logwood and mahogany, there were cheerful, smiling faces
in the counting-houses, and bustle and activity around
the wharves of Belize—when prices fell there was
dullness everywhere; lounging woodcutters on the
bridge or round the grog-shops, instead of being away
in the woods, axe in hand; clerks eating up their
salaries, and principals looking glum.   For little short
of 200 years the Baymen had reaped a rich harvest,
and the crop is not yet exhausted, were prices only
maintained by better demand.   It was about this year,
1850, that permanent depression of the mahogany
trade may be said to have begun.   Prices not only
fell, but, as the larger trees became more difficult to
find in situations near the creeks and rivers handy to
the port of embarkation, the expense of bringing out
the wood after it was felled and squared was much
increased.   The trade had always been a fluctuating

one, but one good season went against a couple of bad
or indifferent ones: lately, however, the margin for
bad years has become less extended.

"Sub umbra floreo," in allusion to the mahogany-
tree, is the motto gratefully chosen by the colonists,
but it is to the humbler denizen of the forest, the log-
wood-shrub, the colony owes its birth.

The value of the wood is said to have been one of
the many discoveries of things useful made by Sir
Walter Raleigh. On one of his cruises he put in at
Trinidad and, his carpenter requiring lumber, brought
some pieces of mahogany off from shore. According
to an anecdote related in Dickens' *All the Year
Round*, accident first led to its use in the manufacture
of furniture. A Dr. Gibbons, who appears to have
flourished about the end of the seventeenth or beginning of the eighteenth century, happened to have a
brother a captain trading to the West Indies. Some
planks or junks of the wood, brought home by the
West India skipper, were thrown aside in the doctor's
back premises, having been found by the carpenters
too hard to work up. But, a short time after, Mrs.
Gibbons required a candle-box, and the mahogany
slabs were put in requisition. The carpenters employed on this occasion also complained that the hardness of the strange wood turned the edges of their
tools, but the candle-box was made. Induced by the
beauty of the grain, now that he had seen the wood
worked up, Dr. Gibbons had a bureau made of the
mahogany, and the fine colour and exquisite polish
caused this piece of furniture to become an object of
curiosity. Amongst others who came, saw and ad-

I 2

mired it, was the Duchess of Buckingham. She at once gave an order to the carpenter who had made the bureau for Dr. Gibbons, Wollaston, for one like it. Wollaston's fortune was made, and furniture in mahogany became the rage.

This magnificent tree is unequalled by any of the forest giants, when all its qualities are considered : the height of the trunk to the first crutch, the space of ground covered by its roots, the girth, wide spread of its branches, its umbrageous foliage, coupled with the beauty and durability of its grain, and value of its timber. In the present century a tree was cut, by a Mr. Charles Craig of Honduras, the trunk of which yielded a log of fifteen tons' weight. It measured 5168 superficial feet, squaring 57 in. by 64 in. The log was trucked out by Mr. Craig, and the limbs of it would probably, when "manufactured," that is, prepared for shipment, more than pay all expenses.[1] Other Brobdingnags of the woods, it is said, of much larger dimensions, have been shipped from the settlement, but the accounts of them do not rest on the very best authority. Henderson speaks of a legendary tree of his day which he puts down as having given 12,000 superficial feet, realizing 1000*l*.

The mahogany-tree belongs to the class *Decandria monogynia*, and its botanical description is :— "Swietenia nect. tubulosum, 10 dentatum. Caps. lignea 5 valves. Sem. imbricata margine membranacea."

It takes 200 years to arrive at maturity.

The Spaniards first used it in ship-building. We

[1] *Honduras Observer*, 1843.

did not follow their example until the close of the first Napoleon's wars. Reliable returns are not procurable farther back than 1802, when 2,250,000 feet are mentioned as the quantity exported; 1803, 4,500,000 feet; 1805, 6,481000, feet. In 1824 it had kept the same figure; in 1840 it was reduced to 4,500,000 feet, but there had been over-exportation in the few years preceding, and stocks had accumulated in the home markets—in 1837, for example, there were shipped from Belize 8,500,000 feet. The same mistake was made in 1845-46. In the first of these years the returns show 9,919,507 feet, and in 1846 the enormous increase of 13,719,075 feet. A portion of these annual quantities was wood cut outside of the limits. The depression in the years 1848, 1849, 1850, is not difficult to account for. In 1874 the quantity had come down to the old figure of about 6,000,000 feet, and in 1878 lower still, 3,146,582 feet.

The fluctuations in price are perhaps not greater than occur to other foreign staples in the English market, and have been affected by similar causes. Thus, for example, an admiralty board could send the market up at once by advertising for tenders; a change in the taste for furniture to maple or black walnut, would send it down for years. Railway construction gave it a lift from 1835 to 1845. The cessation of that new industry on the same extensive scale, and the introduction of iron in place of wood into the ship-building trade, are accountable for its unremunerative aspect from 1850 till the actual present, when a reversion to its use in furniture in America and Europe is again stimulating prices and production. The price was originally 2*s.* 6*d.* per foot, fell gradually to 1*s.*, and eventually to quotations of 4½*d.* to 7½*d.* In 1847 the quotations in the Liverpool prices current are 5*d.* to 1*s.* 4*d.* It is now (1882) quoted at 5*d.* to 9½*d.*, with fair prospect of these prices being upheld.

The quality of the wood shipped from Honduras has not always demanded the top prices in the home market. St. Domingo mahogany and Campeché logwood would appear to fetch better rates at all times. This does not arise altogether from the absence of wood of superior quality in the colony, at least with regard to mahogany, but from other causes. The wood of the northern district is superior to that cut in the central and southern—the latter districts producing plain, free-grained, splitting wood, applicable only to the coarser manufactures. But as the wood of the north, though easier of access to cut, requires to be transported in large and expensive coasters—at a freight of ten to twelve dollars per 1000 feet— to the port of exportation, it leaves less margin for profit than that of the other two districts, at whose rivers' mouths the vessels can lay and load, as the logs are rafted down to them. Hence greater quantities of the inferior quality have been shipped in the past to obtain speedier profits. Much of the wood shipped at Belize comes from beyond the limits, or is shipped by Belize houses and swells the returns for the colony; as for instance, from the Rivers Montagua, Ulloa, Román and Chimilcon, and is all similar in quality— large-sized but plain through, firm in texture.

It is a mistake to suppose that the supply of mahogany is exhausted. There is plenty of wood, and of the finest quality, although, for reasons already given, the cost of production is very greatly increased since the days when no cattle were necessary to haul the logs out of the woods. While acting to some extent on the principle of killing the goose that laid the golden egg, mahogany firms have not been utterly reckless. The system pursued has been to open a work in one direction, fell the largest trees,—those squaring say upwards of 16 in.—leaving the smaller trees to acquire by growth the requisite dimensions. The work would then be closed for a time—from ten to twenty years, let us say. But beyond these are vast tracks of mahogany-bearing lands, which have not as yet re-echoed the clink of the axe. Let prices be maintained, and capital for the initiation of new operations be forthcoming, and abundance of timber of excellent quality will be forthcoming also.

There are two seasons in which the trees are felled ; one beginning shortly after Christmas, or at the end of the wet season, the other about the middle of August. .

The Christmas holidays, which are usually extended well into the new year, over, the labourers turn their minds to completing arrangements for the ensuing season, and "hiring" commences in earnest.

A form of contract between the parties, called a hiring-sheet, is signed before the police-magistrate, according to the ordinance made and provided, and the labourer is bound until next Christmas—longer, of course, or shorter, if he chooses—to his employer. The gangs for mahogany works are generally from twenty-five to fifty strong, with one or more captains, carpenters, foremen, book-keepers, and, over several works, a manager. The labourers are allowed to take their families with them, and seldom see town again until the season's toil is accomplished. Pork, flour, groceries, clothing for the hands, tools, and reserves necessary, are forwarded up to the banks by pitpans from Belize, and before the dry weather has fairly set in, work begins.

Henderson has compared the excitement attendant on the starting of a mahogany-cutting gang to their season's labour after the holidays, in his time, to a crowded embarkation for a long voyage. During the holidays, the hands have indulged in all kinds of excesses, but that short carnival over, the ensuing nine months are vowed to sobriety and hard work.

The situation of the bank or work, the headquarters of the gang, depends on the operations of an individual called the "hunter," but it must necessarily be on an eligible site on the river. About the month of August, the huntsman or tree-finder starts, machéte in hand, to cut his way through the thick bush to some rising eminence, and, climbing the highest tree he can find, examines the surrounding forest. As at this season of the year, the leaves of the mahogany are of a reddish-yellow tint, they are easily distinguishable by the hunter when making his survey. He is, where the lands he is working are not very clearly defined as to proprietary limits, compelled to proceed craftily, so as not to be overreached, especially in placing his marks for recognition, by a rival. The trees are not found in clumps, but singly, sufficiently adjacent, however, to circumscribe the area of operations about to be under-taken.

The bank on the river being conveniently arranged to his discoveries, a main truck-path is opened up in their direction, with branch paths diverging right and left to the trees selected for felling that season. In determining this part of the year's plans, great judgment is required to avoid cutting paths to trees that will not pay for the time and labour necessary to clear a passage to them.

At the bank are the store-houses, bush-dwellings, cattle-sheds, and "barquadier." The hands spend most of their time away in the bush, only meeting at the banks at certain intervals.

The truck-paths having been properly prepared and levelled—work generally given out in tasks of about 100 yards per man per day to clear—the hands are away in the bush, felling. The axe is applied to the trunk about twelve feet from its base, the axe-men standing on a platform skilfully constructed, and attached to the tree. At the moment of falling, a firm nerve and quick eye is required to avoid accidents, which do sometimes occur. The tree felled, the branches are lopped, and they with the trunk reduced from their rounded to a four-sided form. But there they lie, huge, cumbersome timber-giants, and the river, eight or ten miles off, on whose bosom they are eventually to float, sometimes with a sluggish current, anon at a speed of ten miles an hour.

There are two, or properly speaking, three, modes of hauling the precious logs from the depths of their native forests, and of course it depends entirely on the nature of the country and the distance from navigable waters, which mode has to be adopted. Rolling is the original process, long followed with pecuniary success, before cattle-trucks and truck-paths were found necessary. Sliding on skids is practised where the lie of the country, the ground declining gradually to the bank, will admit the logs being hauled over skids, and it is adopted in bringing out the wood from the branch paths into the main truck-path. Trucking is, of course, where the logs are hoisted on to suitably-constructed vehicles, which run on broad wooden truck-wheels, the hindmost higher than the foremost pair. The three modes of carrying away the logs are frequently combined, a season's cuttings being got out partly by trucking, partly by rolling and sliding. To a gang of forty hands there will be a complement of six trucks, with a team of seven or eight pairs of oxen, and two drivers to each truck. The mahogany logs are elevated on the trucks by inclined platforms, the logs having been sawn into sizes to equalize the loads for the yokes of oxen. Twelve men are told off, in trucking, to load, and sixteen to cut food for the teams and to perform miscellaneous duties on the works.

Night is the time selected for trucking out, and the scene is an animated and characteristic one.

Upon the heavy background of the dense, tropical foliage, the torches carried by the workmen make a flickering clear-obscure, by whose light their dusky forms, naked to the waist, are made phantasmagorically visible, moving round the huge, inert mass of timber as it lies on what may readily be mistaken for a gigantic catafalque, while the patient oxen wait for the

crack of the driver's whip, and the shouts of the gang
break the deathlike stillness of the surrounding forest.
The signal given, the whole rude cavalcade starts off
at a rapid pace, with wild whoopings, crackings, and
shouts, for the river's brink.

The logs once arrived at the bank, they are roughly
squared on the river "barquadier," "manufactured,"
the hands call it; but this work is frequently postponed
until the timber arrives at the river-mouths, where are
more extensive and convenient "barquadiers," especially
when advantage has to be taken of sudden high flood.

The body of the tree, from the size of the timber it
furnishes, is deemed the most valuable; but the limbs,
showing a finer and more variegated grain, are preferred for ornamental purposes. Logs cut in February
and September are liable to split, but this can be ob-
viated by keeping them in deep water.

On the Old River, the logs are floated down independently until they reach the point called the Boom,
twenty-three miles up-river from Belize, where they
are collected, formed according to marks into small
rafts as wanted for shipment, and thence floated to
Belize, to be towed alongside the vessels. Previously
to being shipped, the "butts" and "fans" are sawn
off, the wood further (sometimes entirely) prepared
for shipment, bad wood picked out, and the good
measured by sworn measurers.

The question of measurement has always been a
sore one. Notwithstanding their official position, the
measurements of the sworn measurers of the Bay are
little respected by the measurers of Liverpool and
London. The tare and draft in Liverpool generally

comes to an allowance of every third, in London of every fourth, and in Bristol of every fifth log to the buyer. In American ports the mahogany exporter fares no better.

Mahogany-trees shed annually plenty of seeds, so that the natural supply is kept up.

* * * * *

Logwood belongs to the same class botanically (*Decandria monogynia*) as its gigantic neighbour; order, *Lomentacea, L. hœmatoxylon ;* and is described: calyx quinque particle, five capsuled petals, lanceolate, —semi-locular and bivalved—valves navicular. The stem is crooked, and grows sixteen to twenty-four feet high, seldom thicker than a man's thigh, the branches also crooked and irregular, thorny; leaves winged; and flowers pale-yellow.

The yield of it is almost inexhaustible from Campeché, Honduras, and the West India Islands, as it seeds freely, and can be recut in ten to fifteen years. Its original value was 100*l.* per ton, then 40*l.* ; in 1825, 16*l.* ; and it is now quoted at 5*l.* to 7*l.* Its export from the colony has been pretty uniform : 1713 to 1716, 5740 tons; in 1824, over 4000 tons; in 1874, 9210 tons, and since as much as 13,000 tons in one year. Its shipment, except as the broken stowage with mahogany logs, hardly leaves any margin for profit, but it is a favourable mode of remittance for merchants desirous of saving the exchange. It grows in soft, spongy soils. Its production for shipment requires less capital than mahogany, and is frequently undertaken by small capitalists employing small gangs, who pay a royalty for cutting on the estates. It is generally cut the length of cordwood, three feet. It is brought down the rivers and along the coast in dories, and down the rivers in "bark logs," or floating cradles made of the cabbage-palm.

The other woods shipped are cedar, rosewood, santa maria, braziletta, and fustic, but the list of valuable trees of the region is a very long one. Pitch-pine is found in abundance on the ridges. The sappodilla is a most durable wood for house-posts, &c. The caoutchouc (*Siphonia elastica*) is common in certain districts, and there are minor botanical productions to be referred to hereafter. A collection of the woods of the country in polished specimens attracted great attention at the State Fair of Louisiana, held at New Orleans in 1867. Nevertheless, white pine lumber is imported in large quantities.

CHAPTER XI.

HISTORY FROM 1851 TO 1857.

1851-52. COLONEL FANCOURT was succeeded by Sir Philip Wodehouse, K.C.B. He was presented with the usual address on leaving; and upon the whole he had acted with discretion and tact, if he had employed a temporizing policy. He had certainly carried the colony through a season of great internal discord.

A general meeting of the inhabitants was called to consider propositions for a new constitution, which were agreed to and forwarded with a memorial to the Secretary of State for the Colonies, but the wish was not granted for two years after. An act for the better registration of deeds and documents was passed.

The decay of the prosperity of the mahogany and logwood interests led the attention of the far-seeing to be turned to the introduction of other industries, and agriculture was ably recommended in a series of papers by a writer under the signature of "Agricola" in the newspapers.

Sugar-cane. The sugar-cane is indigenous; the soil in localities admirably adapted to its growth, the canes reaching a height of ten, twenty, even thirty feet, and ratooning freely for a decade. In 1847 cane cultivation was introduced into the northern district by the Spanish Yucatecans who had fled thither from the Indians during the outbreak of the war of races. The success these ",rancheritos" met with, although, their capital being small, their operations were limited to the supply of the home demand, led to others embarking in the cultivation.

A sugar-estate was advertised for sale at Manatee in 1847 by J. McDonald. The names of Mr. James Hume Blake and John Johnston are also mentioned in connexion with early sugar-planting. Mr. Carmichael, formerly a Liverpool merchant, became a planter at Corozal, and was the first to persist in the attempt in sugar-planting on a large scale. Twelve estates were started, but upon all of them the same reckless management and want of practical experience were noticeable. Extravagant outlay on machinery and in the introduction of labour resulted in failure and collapse, but most of the estates have changed hands lately, and under different management promise fairly. Experience has been paid for by the pioneers in this attempt, and the lesson of circumspection inculcated, in place of visionary experiments by new beginners.

It would be folly to overlook the fact that, before sugar can be cultivated, the lands have to be cleared. But to counterbalance this, there is the richness of the virgin soil, whose yield—two to three and a half tons per acre—is not surpassed elsewhere. And it must be remembered that the land once cleared, the cost of that in particular is over, while it is generally lessened also, for the canes once established will ratoon with little care for ten years. Here the cleaning should take place from September to November, the planting in June or December. No manuring is required, or likely to be required for an indefinite period. What is wanted is experience and capital. Ten pounds per acre is a fair estimate for the expense of clearing, planting, and keeping clean, for the first year. In the following years the cost of labour for such purposes would be rather less than it is in the islands. Roads can be constructed for about fifty dollars a mile. An advantage too lies in the fact that, whereas, in older sugar-growing countries, the cane trash, or "megass," as it is called— the refuse of the cane after the juice has been expressed —is required for manure, here it will be available for years to come as fuel, and when no longer so, fuel is to be obtained in unlimited supplies to keep the machinery going. Concretors have been introduced and "Honduras Concrete" fetches 19s. to 21s. in the London market; in the United States still higher prices. The first shipment of concrete took place in May, 1867. Muscovado has only a limited market. "From all I have been able to gather," writes the present colonial secretary, "I think it can be demonstrated that well-managed estates in the colony have been able to pay their way, and persons judiciously managing their own estates have been able to make a good living out of them, besides adding to a reserved fund, or reimbursing a fair portion of the purchase-money within a very short time, even under recent adverse circumstances affecting the sugar trade. Whether estates can be continued with the same results will of course depend upon the state of the market." There are advocates of the central factory system, which provides that one class of agriculturalists should grow the canes, and that the results of their labours should be manufactured in a central factory, as English farmers send their wheat elsewhere to be converted into bread. Rum, of course, is produced, but not exported, except in small quantities. It may be smuggled across the frontiers.

As far back as 1807, both sugar and rum, said to be equal to Jamaica, were produced by the settlers on Black River on the Mosquito Shore (Henderson).

The future expectation is that sugar, tobacco, and coffee, with a few other articles, will supplement, if they do not supplant, the older staples ; while large tracts of land, incapable of producing anything else, will yield millions of cocoa-nuts ; richer arable patches being devoted to other tropical fruits for the American markets. It is possible, however, that woods, such as at present are, always will be, exported from Honduras so long as it is a colony of Great Britain.

One of the first matters Sir Philip Wodehouse directed his attention to, was the improvement of the finances and fiscal reform. The colonial secretary was made collector of customs, and that department was rendered more efficient. The most respectable merchants had previously regarded the systematic defrauding of the revenue as a very venial sin.

An anecdote, if not quite proved, is generally believed, that an old lady, purchasing a barrel of flour at a well-known store, was both surprised and delighted to find in the centre of it a neat little quarter-chest of the best Bohea ! *Verb. sap.*

At this time Ruatan was included in the superintendent's commission.

K

1853.   Further attempts at mediation between the contending races, were rejected by the Indian chiefs.

The great event of the year was the remodelling of the constitution by " an act to amend the system of government of British Honduras." It was provided that the executive should consist of a superintendent and a legislative assembly of eighteen elected and three nominated members. The qualification for a vote was fixed at the ownership of real estate of the annual value of 7*l.* sterling, the occupation of land or houses at the annual rental of 7*l.* sterling, or receipt of an annual salary of 100*l.* per annum, both for a period of six months prior to registration. An executive council, composed of the officer commanding the troops, the colonial secretary, the treasurer, attorney-general, and three others chosen by the superintendent, was to assist the superintendent. It was finally established that the judiciary should consist of a chief justice and five assistant-judges, a police-magistrate, coroner, and justices of the peace, with various subordinate public officials.

1853. Imports—198,186*l.*   Exports—345,376*l.*
  „   Revenue—29,510*l.*—Expenditure—28,874*l.*

1854.   A destructive fire broke out this year, on the premises of a Mr. Deiseldorff, who kept a store near the Belize Market, from the ignition of some carpenter's shavings. Damage, confined to the buildings near the market, was done to the amount of 60,000*l.* Contributions were nevertheless sent to the Crimean Patriotic Fund, although that campaign further reduced the demand for the colony's staple products.

1856   Another great fire devastated the north side of the

town of Belize, doing extensive damage to the property of the largest firm in the colony.

This fire was supposed to have been the act of an incendiary, and in the excited state of public feeling, amounting to a panic, a person named Ambrister was imprisoned and tried, found guilty and hung, on the most unsatisfactory evidence. A perusal of the proceedings reflects anything but credit on the prosecution or the judges, and the man was in fact judicially murdered. The common belief is, now, that the principal witness against Ambrister, a miscreant called "Coolie George," incarcerated for other crimes, was deeply perjured, and himself not innocent of this and less destructive arsons.

The following returns of sugar and rum are extracted from the *Official Gazette* of 3rd July, 1856, for the six months ending 31st June of that year :—

Spirits, 14,819 gallons. Sugar, 302,382 lbs.

The Chichenha Indians invaded the territory, thus breaking the long spell of freedom from external attack which since 1798 had been enjoyed by the settlement.

They would appear to have been instigated by the Yucatecan Spaniards, whom they had joined against the Santa Cruz tribe, and who bore us enmity on the grounds of our trading with their inveterate enemies, the same Santa Cruz, in arms and ammunition, which the Belize merchants undoubtedly did and still do, a sale of worthless arms having been made to the chiefs of the Santa Cruz by a large Belize house only last year (1880). Certainly, if strict neutrality is incumbent on any nation in a conflict carried on between a civilized race and warlike savages on its borders, it is incumbent on us, and particularly on our colonial fellow-subjects, when we consider for how long we have carried on similar contests, in various parts of the globe, against aboriginal tribes; and the trade in contraband of war with savages is disgraceful to the Belize firms who profit by it for the time, but eventually suffer with their fellow-colonists, and reprehensible in the executive which winks at such proceedings.

The invaders came across at Blue Creek, on the Hondo (Panting's Bank) and seized and occupied the mahogany works of Messrs. Young, Toledo, and Co., in charge of Mr. Panting. Eventually the firm had to pay a large sum of money to the Indians, to ransom their works, people, and cattle. Notwithstanding that they paid a heavy rent to the Mexican Government for permission to cut mahogany, &c., on Mexican

1857. lands and the Hondo, a second seizure was made of their property on these lands next year by the opposite belligerents, the Santa Cruz. Mr. Edward Rhys of Belize proceeded to Bacalar, and the Santa Cruz made apologies and gave expression to friendly intentions.

1858. Mr. Seymour, Supt. Bacalar was recaptured by the Indians, and the war of castes broke out once more with great fury.

A Captain Anderson and Mr. Blake, a northern planter, went to Bacalar to intercede for and ransom some Spanish prisoners taken by the Indians. They have described the consultation of the "Santa Cruz" oracle, which differs little from similar savage mummeries amongst other superstitious tribes. The oracle

was unpropitious, and the prisoners were massacred
before the eyes of the mediators; the ransom being,
however, honourably returned to Blake. Only the
female children were spared.

A display of force was made by our military
authorities, reinforcements having been applied for
and received from Jamaica. Troops were stationed on
the Hondo, and the Santa Cruz became more friendly
than ever.

In 1860 the Bay Islands were surrendered to the
republic of Spanish Honduras. An act was passed to
legitimize children born out of wedlock on the subsequent marriage of the parents, but the act did not
apply to parties who had ceased to cohabit after the
birth of the children to be legitimized.

1860.
T. Pine,
Acting
Supt.

Permission granted to the state of Guatemala to fit
out vessels and recruit men for operations against the
American Filibustering Expedition.

Registration of Land Titles Act. With reference to
purchases or grants of lands from the crown, " the
practice is not to give a grant now to the purchaser,
but merely to give a receipt for the purchase-money
and to transfer the lands to the buyer upon the records
of the court. Thereupon a certificate is handed to the
buyer, showing on its face the several conveyances of
the estate from the first crown grant to the date of
the purchase." [1] Crown leases of land are granted for
ninety-nine years.

1861.

Two officers, Lieutenants Twigg, R.E., and Plum-
ridge, 3rd West India Regiment, were despatched on
some friendly mission to Bacalar. They would appear to

[1] *British Honduras Colonist,* January, 1868.

have been rather jocularly inclined, and indiscreet in their communications with the chiefs, and were in consequence treated by Benancio Puc or Pec, the Indian comandante, with great indignities. Report speaks of their being put through some painful ordeals with which Chili peppers had something to do, but the officers eventually returned to Belize crest-fallen, but not much the worse corporeally—sadder, but certainly much wiser men.

Population, 25,635.

1862.
Acting
Governor.

In 1862 the settlement was proclaimed a colony, the superintendent in future to be styled Lieutenant-Governor under the Governor of Jamaica.

1863.
Acting
Governor.

Another great fire occurred this year on the south side of the town of Belize.

The Santa Cruz Indians severely chastised the Chichenhas of Icaiché on our borders.

1864-65.

The insurrection of negroes in St. Thomas in the East, Jamaica, broke out prematurely in October of 1865.

J. Gardiner
Austin,
Lieut.-
Governor.

The Chichenhas (Icaiché branch) now became very troublesome to the colony's northern inhabitants, demanding rent which was irregularly paid them by Belize firms who were cutting on the territory between the Rio Bravo and another branch of the Hondo, claimed both by us and the Mexicans. The source of the Hondo formed the basis of the dispute. In 1865 they attacked Quam (or Qualon Hill) on the Bravo, under a chief called Marcos Canul, and carried away the manager, some sixty labourers, and the cattle.

1866.

This gang was ransomed by the government of the colony for 3000*l*. Mr. Phillip's bank at Labouring

Creek was similarly visited a short time after, and at the same time Messrs. Toledo's works at Orange Walk, Old River, had to be abandoned in consequence of their threatening appearance there, making renewed demands for rent.

After much delay a hybrid expedition was organized between Governor Austin and the officer in command of the troops. The governor appointed a civil commissioner (the same Mr. Rhys who had proceeded on a mission to Bacalar in 1856-57). The military comprised the entire garrison of Belize.

One hundred and forty-three men with three officers of the 4th West India Regiment, a volunteer officer who was also an *employé* of Messrs. Toledo and Co., a civilian doctor, and a commissariat-officer, were despatched, as escort to the commissioner and to enforce his demands, up the Old River to Orange Walk in pitpans, carrying with them the requisite supplies and *matériel*, in December, 1866. The force reached Orange Walk in eight days. Another body of troops, composed of a detachment of the 4th West India Regiment under the orders of Captain Edmunds, and a party of volunteers, proceeded in a small steamer to the Hondo, to intercept the Indians should they attempt to cross that frontier. The Old River expedition was militarily commanded by Major Mackay, 4th West India Regiment, and having crossed the Belize, marched at midnight upon an Indian village, San Pedro de Siris, within our limits; the comandante of which was one Asencion Ek. The route was by an abandoned truck-path, crossed by enormous creeks and knee-deep in mud, the season being the

wet one. The men were soon exhausted, and the
loaded mules "bogged" at every creek. After a
toilsome and harassing night-march, the troops
halted at daylight for breakfast, and while so engaged
the head of the column was suddenly attacked by a
party of Indians. It has been attempted to prove
that the Indians were insignificant as to numbers.
Sufficient discredit attaches to the affair without
minimizing the enemy's force, but, although from their
peculiar bush-tactics no approximate idea even of
their numbers could be formed, they must have been
in force, as in the short brush which ensued, lasting
about twenty minutes, four men of the 4th West India
Regiment and two carriers were killed, and sixteen
others wounded.

For some reason best known to himself Major
Mackay ordered the bugler to sound the retire about
twenty minutes after the first shot was fired. The
troops at first obeyed the order reluctantly, but as the
three combatant officers, the gallant major at their
head, nobly led the strategic movement to the rear,
the retreat soon became a stampede back along the
line of the previous night's march, during which the
black troops threw away everything but their rifles
and pouches. The truck-path was strewn with water-
proof sheets, haversacks, &c., &c. ; the medical pan-
niers, ammunition, and commissariat stores, including
a rocket-gun (6-pounder), were abandoned, and mules
and horses galloped home alone. The Indians had also
taken to their heels. Arrived at Orange Walk, Major
Mackay called a council of war, to which he summoned
besides his two subaltern officers, the volunteer and

commissariat-officers, and the civilian doctor also gave his opinion. The men, it was found, were in a state of mutiny, openly cursing the major. They had fired off all the ammunition in their pouches save a few rounds ; they were shoeless; the rest of the ammunition, and the commissariat and medical supplies were lost ; there were no means of transport to resume the march with, and, worst of all, all confidence in the commanding officer was gone. A return to Belize by river was decided upon, and immediately carried out.

The commissioner, Mr. Rhys, disappeared at the moment the cry of "Indians !" was raised during the memorable halt for breakfast, and his subsequent fate was never cleared up. He was well known to the Indians—indeed, had a good deal of Indian blood in him by his mother's side—and it is supposed if they recognized him they would do him no harm. He was in delicate health and almost a cripple, and it is most likely he got separated from the main party during the encounter, and, from the subsequent hasty retreat, could not succeed in rejoining it, but eventually perished in the bush. He was the son of a retired army-doctor who had settled and married in the colony, and was a gentlemen of considerable ability, great courage and firmness and amiability.

The news of the disaster preceded the troops to Belize, where the greatest excitement and apprehension prevailed. The volunteers were kept on duty day and night, the Indians being looked for either ahead of, or in the immediate wake of Mackay and his routed Zouaves.[2]

The Hondo party, under Captain Edmunds, which

[2] The West India corps wear the Zouave dress.

had reached Betson's Bank on that river, was recalled, and the inhabitants, Governor Austin's family, at least, included, if not himself, were all packed up ready to take to the shipping.

Dr. Hunter of Belize, public medical officer, who accompanied Captain Edmunds' party, speaks well of the cheerfulness with which the volunteers submitted to the hardships of a bush-campaign.

A court of inquiry was subsequently held on Major Mackay. He was leniently allowed to sell out, notwithstanding that at Tubebarcalong in Africa he had been previously reported by Governor D'Arcy for "tardiness" in meeting the enemy. Let us be lenient too, and allow him his own excuse, "he lost his head;" a heart in his breast he never had to lose. Christmas was anything but a holiday in Belize that year.

1867.
J. R. Longden, Lieut.-Governor.

The opening of the year following brought one man-of-war after another to the harbour of Belize. The garrison of Belize was reinforced by 300 of the 3rd West India Regiment under Lieutenant-Colonel Harley, a 6-pounder Armstrong, and a party of white artillerymen from Port Royal.

In February a second expedition started by a different route to Old Orange Walk, and the district of the recent disaster (as subsequently was the Hondo district) was scoured by the flying column, without the foe being encountered, or greater military achievements accomplished than the burning of the aforesaid San Pedro de Siris, and other Indian villages. As Mr. Fowler correctly describes it in his rapid sketch already alluded to, the operations were rather of the "Bombastes Furioso" order.

CHAPTER XII.

THREE years after Lieutenant-Colonel Harley's grand 1868
campaign, Canul and Chan, two chiefs of the Icaichés,
marched through the country to Corozal, and took
possession of it, asking for an interview with the magistrates, from whom Canul peremptorily demanded payment of $3000, as a penalty for the inhabitants having
supplied their enemies with arms and ammunition.
But some of the Santa Cruz Indians happened to
appear upon the scene, and Canul, fearing they would
bring their tribe upon him, withdrew his force, said
to number 400. Mr. Longden, the lieutenant-
governor, took prompt measures for defence. But in
1872 the same Canul attacked Orange Walk, New
River, in earnest, and was repulsed by the detachment
of troops under Lieutenant Smith, 1st West India Regiment, who was seriously wounded. Fourteen men
were wounded and two killed—a Yucatecan was bar-
barously killed—and some twenty-five or thirty of the
inhabitants wounded; fifteen houses were burnt, and
others pillaged. A useful diversion was created by
some American settlers (accustomed to Indian raids
probably). One of them, Mr. Oswald, received the
Cross of St. Michael and St. George. Canul was

killed, and since that time the colony has been free from Indian incursions. The war of races still continues in Yucatan.

The "Indios bravos," or unsubdued indigenous tribes of Yucatan, are trained to arms and discipline, are capable of enduring much fatigue, and, though invariably low in stature, are wiry, hardy, and courageous. They are badly armed with old smooth-bores, and ill provided with ammunition, using any small pellet of iron and buck-shot in place of the bullet. They follow the ordinary bush-tactics of savage tribes, and invariably carry a machéte or cutlass. They wear white linen or duck suits and straw hats, brown leather accoutrements and moccasins. On the march they roll their trousers above the knee, and carry with them their simple rations of corn-cakes or tortillas.

1872-78. As these events produced a diplomatic correspondence between the British and Mexican Governments which in its progress entered upon the question of territorial rights, it may be appropriate to consider it in this place. The first despatch is from Lord Granville, and is under date 2nd of March, 1872. After detailing the recent attack by Canul at Orange Walk, and alluding to the other incursion into the colony in 1870, the British minister directs the attention of the Mexican authorities to the matter, and claims "satisfaction for the past and security for the future." The reply from the Mexican Foreign Office is signed by J. M. Lafragua, and dated 12th of February, 1873. In it is denied the control over Canul by the Government of Mexico, and all responsibility, directly or indirectly, for the acts of that chief, or the Chichenha Indians. It also retorts

upon us that the colonists of Belize have fomented
the war of races in Yucatan, and remarks, "Esta
guerra no ataca el derecho de gentes, sino la justicia
universal; no viola un tratado, sino la moral; no ofende
á un pueblo, sino á la humanidad." This is replied to
by Lord Derby in a despatch of the 28th of July, 1874,
in which he incontestably proves that Marcos Canul,
his predecessor Puc, and his successor Chan, were recognized as generals and comandantes of the canton
of Icaiché, both by the Comandante of Bacalar,
and the Governor of Campeché, and refers to despatches
and official documents in support. Lord Derby reiterates
the demand for indemnification made by Lord Granville in 1872, and that efficacious measures should be
taken by the Mexican Government against a repetition
of similar invasions. A change also having taken
place in the *personnel* of the Mexican Foreign Office,
Lord Derby's note is replied to by H.E. Señor Vallarta in a very long and very able despatch, dated
23rd of March, 1878. Señor Vallarta rather springs a
mine under the British Foreign Office by taking his
start from the Treaty of Versailles, 1783, and the Convention of London, 1786, between Great Britain and
Spain; "posteriamente revividos" by the Treaties of
Amiens, 1802, and Madrid, 1814, as he alleges. He
alludes for a confirmation to a correspondence between
the Governor of Bacalar, Don Juan Bautista Gual, in
1810 and 1812, with Lieutenant-Colonel Nugent Smyth,
then Superintendent of British Honduras, in which the
Mexican official contends against the arguments of
English writers, that the colony was not comprehended
in the provisions of those treaties (1802 and 1814), ex-

cept as regards the mere defining of existing boundaries, and their assertion of the point that England,
by her colonial subjects settled in Honduras, had
acquired a title to sovereignty over it by right of conquest in 1798. He also alleges that the "leyes del
parlemento inglés de 1817 y 1819" confirm categori-
cally and determinately that Belize "no está dentro de
los limites y dominos de S. M. B.," and the English
Parliament by these "leyes" had declined to assume
the right to legislate for Honduras, except under the
stipulations of the treaty of 1783 and convention of
1786.

The Mexican Foreign Minister's further arguments
may be epitomized thus, that by the Treaty of London,
26th December, 1826—framed purposely for the formal
recognition of Mexican independence—all the rights,
territorial and otherwise, held by Spain at the time of
the declaration of independence of Mexico, and
anterior to that political event, devolved upon the
Mexican Government. And Señor Vallarta goes on to
catalogue the various subsequent occasions which have
given rise to discussion between Great Britain and
Spain—in 1812-13 on the question of limits; and with
Mexico as to her pretensions, in 1826, 1828, 1849,
in which the terms of the treaties made with Spain
are alleged to have been invariably recognized as
still binding and as the basis of negotiations by the
British representatives. Moreover, that at the pre-
liminary negotiations for a treaty of amity and for
recognition between Spain and Mexico, 1835, Mr.
Villiers, our minister at Madrid, demanded a formal
cession from Spain of British Honduras; which ces-

sion would not have been demanded had we then considered we possessed sovereign rights over the territory. The treaty of 1836, by which Spain finally recognized Mexico, further confirms to her territorial rights, Señor Vallarta argues, over the colony of British Honduras; and with allusion to subsequent correspondence, he closes what must be considered an ingeniously-put case, by saying,—

" The recognition of the independence of the republic transfers to it legally the sovereign rights which Spain had exercised over it (British Honduras) by right of conquest."

It is not difficult to meet Señor Vallarta's arguments. It cannot, to begin with, be granted that in all cases where a change in the form of government, or a transfer of the governing power to other hands, has taken place, the treaty rights of the former holder of sovereign power necessarily devolve upon the successor. A treaty is a solemn engagement between two (or more) high contracting parties, described in the preamble with minute and technical precision. Without the acquiesence of both England and Spain, Mexico could not assume the place of Spain in a treaty between them, affecting their respective interests, and binding them alone. Nor was Mexico ever in the position to assume any of the territorial rights of Spain, but as a revolted subject dependency had to make good her title *vi et armis* to the territory actually in her possession, until Spain executed the treaty of 1836, and thus recognized her independence; her very existence previously being due to revolutionary proceedings, which Spain, theoretically, at all events, refused to acknowledge or countenance until 1835, the date of treaty negotiations ; Spain having still the right to reduce Mexico again to subjection up to that date by force of arms.

We must get behind the treaty of 1826, by which Great Britain recognized Mexican independence—and almost contemporaneously that of the other revolted Spanish republics—to the date of the revolts and declarations of independence. Here was a complete *bouleversement* of existing affairs, not a mere transfer of power and sovereignty to which the *de jure* party in possession, Spain, gave consent to the assumption of her rights by those who were in *de facto* possession. *We* had in fact a better title to our territory in Central America, than any of the new republics who in international law had as yet no *locus standi* and no title, other than the "nine points of law"—one of actual possession —until formally recognized by Spain and other powers.

It was therefore, and is, only Spain herself whom we could ever have recognized as possessing a shadow of right to a title to the territory we claim, or a right to dispute ours. But Spain had abandoned all claim, and given tacit consent to the exercise by us of all the rights of sovereignty she had by previous treaties denied us up to 1798, and had she even felt disposed to transfer her rights, had no longer the power to do so. Since the defeat of the Spaniards under Marshal O'Neil by the settlers, plantations had been formed ; crown grants of land made ; fortifications erected ; a superintendent appointed by royal letters patent ; regular troops stationed permanently, and barracks built ; and consuls had been appointed by the new Spanish republics, and by Mexico herself. Further, the settlers no longer confined their operations to the limits laid down by former treaties, but acted contrary to the express stipulations of them by occupying the district from the Sibun to the Sarstoon in addition to what they had already occupied so long.

These encroachments were neither resented nor objected to by Spain, on pacific relations between the two powers being resumed at the close of the war which had broken out in 1796, nor was any remonstrance lodged by Spain against them, or any assumption of sovereign rights, between the dates of the Treaty of Paris (1814) and the revolt of the Spanish American provinces.

The treaties between Spain and England of 1802 and 1814, by which Señor Vallarta claims the older treaties executed previous to 1798 are renewed (*revividos*), do not refer to the subject at all, but they contemplate "the early negotiation of a new treaty of commerce at a fitting time."

The laws of the British Parliament ("leyes del parlamento inglés de 1817-19.") referred to by the Mexican Foreign Minister, are 57 George III. cap. 53, and 59 George III. cap. 44. They provide for the punishment of murders, &c., committed in Honduras and other places "not within his Majesty's dominions," but so far from renouncing the right to legislate for Honduras, assert it, and provide for the execution of it. These acts were necessary, because, first, Honduras was then a settlement, not a colony, therefore strictly speaking, not within his Majesty's dominions, as Ireland, or Jamaica even. Second, the sovereignty *de jure* was vested by treaty in Spain, but *de facto* exercised by the British settlers. And third, Spain having been since the Peninsular war an ally of Great Britain, and on friendly terms, it was not likely England would wound her susceptibilities in this matter. But Spain had previously, and did then and subsequently, allow her claims of sovereignty to go by default as has been set forth above, and more especially by the cessation of the exercise of her treaty right to send commissioners into the colony after the attack on St. George's Caye, and her general indifference to the course pursued by the British Government, although approached on the subject in 1835.

When it was proposed, in 1862, to declare the settlement a colony, Spain was communicated with, but no remonstrance was forthcoming, and this communication to the court of Madrid shows that Spain, and Spain alone, was considered as possessing at any time a right to be consulted, which right she has forfeited all claim to—except one on the diplomatic courtesy of Great Britain—by her own lapses.

The only protest lodged was one by the American consul, bribed, it is said to make his country look ridiculous, or imbued with the spirit of the Monroe doctrine, and anxious to shine before his little world.[1]

British Honduras is excepted from the conditions of the Clayton-Bulwer Treaty, which promises, on the part of Great Britain, not to colonize Nicaragua, Central America, and the Mosquito Coast.

It is clear that neither Mexico nor the Central American States knew their proper territorial limits when they revolted. The federal constitution of

[1] See Whitaker's Almanac, 1879, page 249.

Mexico, promulgated October 4, 1824, states that " the limits of the confederation shall be defined by a constitutional law as soon as circumstances permit." Also the federal constitution of the Central American States, promulgated November 22nd, 1824, states that " the limits of the territory of the states shall ·be defined by a constitutional law when the necessary information shall have been obtained."

These constitutional laws have not been passed as yet.

In 1827 Mexico appointed commissioners to ascertain the limits between herself and Guatemala, and to inspect the boundary-line of the British settlement, and the step was preparatory to the Mexican Government inviting the British Government to appoint a commission to carry into effect article xiv. of the treaty between Mexico and Great Britain of December 26th, 1826, to settle the limits claimed by the British settlers, who, it was well known at that time, had passed the limits fixed by the Convention of London of 1786.

The treaty of 1826, art. xiv., " reserves the rights, privileges and immunities of H.B. Majesty's subjects within the limits laid down in the convention of 14th July, 1786, the contracting parties to the treaty reserving for some more fitting opportunity the further arrangements on the article." This is interpreted by Mexico as implying a recognition of its succession to the rights of the crown of Spain, and the reservation of the rights of the British settlers within the limits of the convention of 1786. But on what principle could Great Britain recognize such rights in the republic of Mexico in face of treaties with Spain,

unless her treaties with that power had been specifically abrogated, and Mexico previously placed in the
stead of Spain?

That Spain was approached in 1835 by our minister
at Madrid shows conclusively that we never recognized
any rights beyond our own, except hers.   Nor was it
likely England would jeopardize the interests of her
own subjects who had thrown off the yoke of Spain
more than twenty years before Mexico did so (1821)
under her ephemeral Emperor Iturbide, and who had
rights of occupation existing over two hundred years,
which had been time after time recognized by Spain
by treaty engagements.

The " fitting opportunity " for making further
arrangements on article xiv. of the treaty of 1826,
like the making of the constitutional law to define
boundaries has not yet come, it would appear.

The British settlers established the same rights in
1798 over the territory they occupied, that Mexico did
in 1821 over the territory the Mexican revolutionary
leaders controlled; therefore British Honduras was a
state twenty years old, before the republic of Mexico
had any existence.

Mexico claims the sovereignty exercised by Spain
over British Honduras under the treaty of 1836, a
sovereignty which had *de facto* ceased for more than a
quarter of a century previously.   Let it even have
been supposed to exist *de jure* at the recognition of
Mexico by Spain by that treaty of 1836, Spain could
not transfer it in face of the treaties of 1783-86, without
the consent of England.   Spain, if she had included a
transfer of sovereignty over British Honduras and the

British subjects of that territory in her treaty recognizing her revolted province, Mexico, would have committed an overt act of hostility against a faithful ally; an act which if Spain were now accused of she would disown, and of which any European government would be ashamed.

It is not likely that arguments apparently strong, but intrinsically so weak as Señor Vallarta's will be used except as a set-off to similar claims by us for Indian raids.

Against the arguments that the Mexican Government is not responsible for the acts of the Indians still unsubdued; that our lieutenant-governors have entered into compacts with their chiefs; and that our colonists have supplied arms and powder to tribes hostile to Mexico, we fear it will not be such an easy matter to furnish replies.

Since penning the above, we have accidentally come across a short correspondence quietly ignored by Señor Vallarta, from which we make the following extracts :—

1. "Her Britannic Majesty's Envoy Extraordinary and Minister Plenipotentiary to Mexico, to H.E. Señor Ramirez :—

"*Mexico, March 6th*, 1865.

"The undersigned has the honour, &c.; that the attention of H.M. government has been drawn to a proclamation or decree issued by certain commissioners of the Emperor of Mexico on 19th September last, and published in the "Gazette of Yucatan," of the 23rd of that month, wherein the boundaries of the province of Yucatan are treated in such a manner as to comprise within its limits the British colony of Honduras. The undersigned is ordered formally to declare to the Mexican Minister for Foreign Affairs on the part of her Majesty's Government, and does hereby declare, that Mexico has no claim whatever to any part of the territory which forms the colony of British Honduras, which is under the exclusive sovereignty of the British crown."

"The undersigned, &c.,

"P. C. SCARLETT."

2. H.E. Señor Ramirez to our envoy in reply :—

" *Mexico, March 9th*, 1865.

[After acknowledging receipt, &c.] "In his turn has the satisfaction to declare to her Britannic Majesty's Minister that there must be some error in the case, as Mexico has never enunciated the pretensions indicated. If anything has been done to the contrary, the emperor's government will correct it immediately ; as it is jealous of the inviolability of its frontiers, so will it religiously respect that of its neighbours. The undersigned hopes to have the pleasure of giving to Mr. Scarlett explanations which should suffice to remove all doubts, on seeing the antecedents of the affair."

1867-68. Having brought the accounts of the Indian raids down to the last instance, it is necessary to catch up the thread of the general history where it was dropped.

1867.
Lieut.-
Governor
Longden.

The finances of the colony, heavily burdened by the payment of the military expenses incurred by the operations of 1866-67, were in a deplorable condition when taken in hand by Mr. Longden. An act was passed to levy a land-tax.

Sir John Peter Grant, the Governor of Jamaica and dependencies, of which the colony was one, paid it a visit—the first instance of such an event. The general commanding, Major-General Luke Smyth O'Connor, also renewed his acquaintance with the colony in which he had formerly served, by visiting it on a tour of military inspection.

During " the reconstruction " of the Southern States of America after the civil war, a portion of the dissatisfied ex-confederates found their way to British Hon-. duras, but advantages were not held out to them, and only a proportion of them eventually became settlers. One hundred arrived first in the steamer *Trade-Wind*. It is alleged that the late Governor Mr. Austin's sudden and undignified removal from his post, was due to the unauthorized grants by him of crown lands at a cheap rate to these Southern exiles, rather than to his recent mismanagement of Indian affairs. Our home government probably did not wish to offend that of the United States by offering inducements to its malcontent subjects to leave their own country for one of our colonies.

Two hundred more of these planters, however, some with capital, arrived the year following. 1868.

A frontier police-force was organized, which was shortly disbanded.

A certain number of the American families from the Southern States about this time obtained lands on tolerably easy terms from the house of Toledo and Co., and settled about a mile north of the Carib village of Punta Gorda, almost on the southern border; built houses, made four miles of road, a wharf, dug wells, and resolutely set to work to clear away the bush.   There were originally sixty souls belonging to the " Hatch," (a Wesleyan) community, but they have from one cause or another dwindled down to a few families. They commenced the cultivation of sugar, and by great perseverance the remnant have thrived by sup-plying the home market.   According to the Hon. H. Fowler, they had 240 acres under cultivation in 1878. They had little or no capital, and furnish a striking instance of what energy and perseverance can accom-plish in the colony when properly directed.   The Rev. Levi Pearce has been perhaps the most successful amongst them.   He is a gentleman of superior attain-ments, somewhat advanced in years, but did not disdain to cast off his coat and join his sons, axe in hand.

1869.   The *Trade-Wind,* the steamer carrying the mails to New Orleans, was lost.

This year the colony took what all lovers of liberty and free institutions must consider a retrograde step. The legislative assembly committed political suicide by petitioning that Honduras, like Jamaica, whose constitution was altered after the disastrous events of 1865, should be made a crown colony.   In the case of this colony there was no occasion for this movement, and bitterly are the inhabitants now rueing it, that they allowed a majority of their representatives to throw the colony back in its political career.

1870.
W. W.
Cairns,
Lieut.-
Governor.

The Indian troubles having been brought down to 1872, there remains little of historical interest to add to the account of the colony.   In 1870 it became a crown colony, after having enjoyed free representative institutions, in one form or another, for 200 years from its origin in 1670.

During the administration of affairs by Mr. Cairns— including the period when Lieutenant-Colonel Harley acted for the lieutenant-governor on leave—the measures of retrenchment initiated by Mr. Longden were carried on, and the colony felt little or no change from its altered constitution ; while general affairs assumed a more healthy condition. 1871. Lient.-Col. Harley acting for Mr.Cairns.

The census of 1871 showed the population to have increased considerably.

	Males.	Females.	Total.
Northern District	5577	4975	10,552
Central „	5398	5510	10,908
Southern „	1628	1622	3,250
	12,603	12,107	24,710

The difficulty of taking the census is very great, but the returns are probably under rather than over the actual numbers.

In 1872 Mr. Cairns resumed his post. Captain Mitchell, R.M., colonial secretary, was acting in 1874 and 1876. Major Mundy arrived as governor in 1874, and retired on a pension in 1876. In 1877 the present governor, F. P. Barlee, C.M.G., took up the reins of government. The advent of irresponsible power was not much felt until the present *régime.* Since 1870 the government of the colony, it must be obvious, has been purely personal, for the executive council and legislative council have no influence. The former composed entirely of officials under the governor, viz. the chief justice, colonial secretary, officer command- 1872-82.

ing the troops, colonial treasurer, and attorney-general, are merely a committee to carry out the views of the governer.   The legislative council, consisting of the above official members, with the addition of five un-official members, nominated by the executive, meets once a year to give formal sanction to the cut and dried measures laid before it.   The nominated mem-bers, if they are inclined to discussion, or any of their number daring opposition, are soon muzzled and driven to retire in disgust.   Such a form of government, it is almost unnecessary to point out, must depend for its character on the temper and proclivities of the one man at the head of it.   In 1880 the inhabitants, feel-ing the curb as tightened upon them by Lieutenant-Governor Barlee unbearable, petitioned the Secretary of State for restitution of self-government; but a Liberal cabinet at home refused the restoration of free institutions to a colony abroad.   Hope is not abandoned that ere long that restoration will be granted.   It pro-bably would have been had Lord Carnarvon been at the Colonial Office when the memorial went home.

The mahogany and logwood trades continued on the whole in a languishing condition during this period, while the sugar trade also received a check from the failure of those who had originally embarked in it without practical experience or sound judgment, and with too high-flown notions.   Sugar cultivation, how-ever, if it is never destined to become the mainstay of the colony's prosperity, will surely one day, and that an early one, develop into a most efficient prop to its welfare.

The rise and progress of the fruit trade followed

on increased means of steam communication with America.

The following statement will give an idea of the fiscal and commercial state of the colony during the period under consideration :—

COMPARATIVE STATEMENT OF RECEIPTS AND EXPENDITURE, &c., 1870-78.

Year.	Revenue.	Expenditure.	Public Debt.	Imports.	Exports.
	£	£	$	$	$
1870	133,617	131,100	147,950	921,685	859,885
1871	189,432	139,833	147,950	903,300	1,038,355
1872	195,681	152,770	111,609	844,045	1,017,860
1873	260,053	182,318	77,950	1,183,075	1,084,960
1874	222,454	200,051	76,950	891,885	1,203,140
1875	213,482	203,923	65,305	876,605	1,102,560
1876	213,716	219,192	25,204	817,015	1,032,100
1877	220,110	217,488	25,204	836,160	622,515
1878	201,807	255,469	25,204	957,453	655,035

The exports, with the exception of one year (1873), show in favour of the colony over the imports, and it must also be taken into consideration that the colony has had a fair import transit trade. The public debt was chiefly for military expenditure, and for the last three years entirely under that head to the imperial government, and has since been almost extinguished.

Year.	Revenue.	Expenditure.	Public Debt.	Imports.	Exports.
	$	$	$	£	£
1879	201,624	253,498	22,529	159,883	187,673
1880	216,172	189,613	44,260	237,204	252,855
1881	218,211	203,569	39,629	201,811	247,402

The bonded and warehousing system has been perfected, but it is less a source of revenue now since the transit trade has been diverted through steamers calling at southern Spanish ports.

In 1878 the old court-house was pulled down, and on the site an expensive pile of public offices (completed 1880) and court-house erected, which has given anything but general satisfaction. The old court-house had lasted since 1818, and the mahogany logs dug out of its foundation only needed to be trimmed to render them fit for sale. This after having been buried sixty years.

During his term of office Governor Cairns suggested the holding of an industrial exhibition. It came off in 1872. [Another was proposed to be held in May of the year 1882.] In that year a stringent press law virtually prevented the establishment of journals other than the *Official Gazette.* Two newspapers have since been started : the *Belize Advertizer* in May, 1881, and the *Colonial Guardian,* January, 1882.

The disestablishment of the Church of England has assimilated the ecclesiastical status of the colony to that of other colonies. It was effected in 1871.

Corozal, the principal place in the northern district, has much increased both in population and the importance of its trade with the neighbouring Spanish countries, and in its manufacture of sugar and rum.

In no department have there been more frequent changes than in the mail route. Since 1879 the royal mail route *viâ* Jamaica has been abandoned, and that *viâ* New Orleans reverted to. The subsidy paid is about the same ($25,000) as formerly, but the service is fortnightly instead of monthly.

Increased intercourse and communications have produced increased material prosperity, but no amelioration in the social features of the population. Concubinage is still preferred to the married state by the lower orders, and immoral connexions between the sexes exist in every grade of society. The leaven of slavery times in the relations of the sexes will probably never be eliminated. Drunkenness is very prevalent, and crimes of violence common. In other crimes the colony contrasts favourably with most communities comparable with it. Little attempt has been made to elevate morals, extend education, or introduce refinement. The inhabitants are as conservative in their bad social, as they were formerly in their excellent political, "usages and customs."

CHAPTER XIII.

VARIOUS ELEMENTS OF THE POPULATION, 1881.

THE census-returns[1] taken this year are probably tolerably near the mark. They are as under,—

	Males.	Females.	Total.	Increase.	
				Total.	Per cent.
Northern District .	6,084	5,355	11,439	877	8·31
Central District .	5,554	5,655	11,209	301	2·75
Southern District .	2,470	2,334	4,804	1554	47·81
	14,108	13,344	27,452	2732	

Showing an enormous increase in the southern district. The white population amounted to 375, 271 of whom were males. Representatives of every nation under the sun are to be found in this peculiar little colony. The phlegmatic German, the volatile Frenchman, the Belgian cross between these two, the morose but imperturbable European Spaniard, contrasting with his colonial counterpart, the hot-blooded Italian, the Swiss, Dane, Swede and Nor-

The varieties of the population.

[1] From official returns in Colonial Secretary's Office.

wegian, occasionally a Russian Finn or a Polander Jew,
and the three varieties of the insular-minded Briton,
all preserving their national traits, if their habits are
modified by tropical customs and the warmth of the
climate. The East sends its bespangled, turbaned,
delicate-featured Hindoo, and "heathen Chinee," cute
and ugly-featured, both indescribably dirty; the latter
chin-chinning with Maya Indians (some mystic affinity
having been discovered mutually between the two
races). Waikas and Caribs are indigenous, and then
there is the vast mixed population of every shade of
colour, every degree of ethnological distinction that
science can invent in order to classify the combinations
natural production on principles of miscegenation has
produced, from the coal-black, cicatrized Eboe or
Mandingo from Guinea, to the sickly-complexioned
mustafina, through all the variations and gradations of
mixed descent—mulatto and sambo, mestizo or ladino,
quadroon, octaroon, and mustee.

The aborigines claim priority in description. The aboriginal tribes as they exist in Central America to-day have not received the attention their numbers and past interesting history (slightly sketched in an early chapter) seem to warrant. *Indians.*

The descendants of the great Toltec nation now to be met with in Honduras, either settled in villages within its boundaries or occasionally visiting the towns to purchase or sell, present many features of a common origin, but, as in the Waikas, who are supposed to have an admixture of African blood, sometimes develop distinctive ethnological features and characteristics. The Indians of Guatemala and Yucatan assimilate more to each other and present in fact but few points of divergence. They are a small-sized, swarthy-complexioned, wiry race, not capable of sustained physical exertions ; Asiatic in feature. Of those still in a wild state little is known. Unreclaimed (*Los Candones,* unbaptized), they roam the wilds of Central America. Certain ferocious tribes, called " Indios bravos "[2] by the Yucatecans and Hondurenos, used formerly to make incursions on the settlements ; but none of these are to be confounded with the semi-civilized yet unsubdued tribes such as the Icaichés and Santa Cruz, inhabiting territory close to our borders.

The Mayas of Yucatan, more isolated in their peninsula, have perhaps preserved the traditions of their race with greater fidelity than other tribes, and are also more warlike. The bow and arrow is still the weapon of such unreclaimed tribes as the " Jicaques " of Honduras, but the Mayas of Yucatan are armed with guns and machétes or cutlasses. The religion of the Mayas, like that of the whole Toltec nation, was a form of idolatry ; but Cogullado, who wrote a history of Yucatan, published at Campeché, 1742, credits them with belief in a supreme deity ruling over their tutelary gods, and an evil spirit, Xibilba ; also in a future state of rewards and punishments. The name of the Santa Cruz tribe, and their ceremonies of the oracle, revive the story, so common with all the monkish historians of the Spanish conquest, of the worship of the symbol of the cross among the aboriginal tribes in Mexico. The Mayas kept on bark leaves a record of events : their chronicles of wars, inundations, hurricanes, famines,

---

[2] Such were and are the Chols Mopan, Jicaques, Poyais, &c.

" y otros sucesos." In their chronology they divided the year into eighteen months of twenty days each. The surplus five days—corresponding to our 12th to 16th July—were considered unpropitious. They also marked lustres of ten, twenty, and forty years by stones wrought and placed in certain positions in the temples. Cogulludo is inclined to think the ruined remains of Yucatan assimilate the Toltec rather than the Aztec specimens of architectural relics, which although evidencing a common origin exhibit divergences from the common type. The worthy padre expresses his curiosity as to who the workmen were who produced these buildings of wrought stone; " piedra labrada ;" and sadly remarks "ni los indios tienen tradicion de ello." The Chevalier Friedrichsthal, a Vienna naturalist, visited the ruins in 1838, combining archæological with botanical research. He identifies the general character of those at Uxmal and Chichen-Itza with those of Palenque, " but," he says, with reference to the ruins of Yucatan, "the stonework of the outside walls is more sumptuous and more neatly finished." He notices the accurate reference to the east in the erection of temples, the concrete foundation of the walls, terraced construction, low elevation, and astonishing variety of hieroglyphs and statuary. He found no trace of Egyptian tile or brick work. Stephens also explored Yucatan and its ruins. He states that " for the first time in Yucatan " he finds at one place only, Chichen-Itza, the character of the sculptured hieroglyphs " beyond all question bearing the same type " as that he previously discovered in the ruined remains formerly met with by him and the artist

M

Catherwood, who accompanied him at Copan and Palenque.

The Indians who are found in the vicinity of Belize—at Peten in Guatemala and at Bacalar in Yucatan, for example—are baptized, but mix up idolatrous rites and superstitious beliefs with the Christian creed and ceremonies. In disposition they are docile and timid and inoffensive, except, as in the case of Chichenhas and Santa Cruz, when roused to take part in a war of races, when they become cruel and fierce. They live industriously and inoffensively in villages scattered over the district, cultivating their patches of maize and pulse, their pigs and poultry—those near the coast engaging in fishing, and cutting braziletto or tinta (logwood), and trading with Belize, and even Havana, in their hollowed-out "bongays" or coasting proas. Their diet is simple and frugal, and rather monotonous, consisting of corn cakes (tortillas), frijoles (fried beans), eggs, and occasionally poultry, game, wild hog dried, or domestic pork. Their dress is equally simple and also light; the ladies wear simply a double allowance of embroidered robe; one depending from the hip to the ankle, the other from the shoulder to a little below the waist. In full dress they wear a shawl after the mode of the Spanish mantilla, and at all times plain gold ornaments, especially ear-rings. The men wear only loose drawers and a shirt or blouse of manta drill or manta cruda, straw hats, and a coloured sash round the waist. Both sexes wear moccasins on their feet. In full dress the men wear pantaloons over the drawers, tuck in the shirt, and wear a braided vest. Mounted, the poncho—called "mango" or "serape" according to style—is carried for wet weather. Men and women are perpetually smoking their " cigaritos " or straw cigarettes. Their houses are erections of wattle and daub (adobe) thatched with palm-leaves. Their intellectual capabilities are by no means slight.

Formerly the Indians of Yucatan were formed into one kingdom, called Mayapan, ruled over by a supreme chief, with subsidiary chiefs under him who were semi-independent. Previous to the Spanish conquest of Mexico, about 1420, the tributary caciques revolted, and the chief ruler was left only the province of Mani. One of these revolted chiefs left his own province of Chichen-Itza, about twenty leagues from Tinhoo, now Merida, and retired to the Lake of Peten (lake of the island) or Itza, fixing his residence on Peten Grande, the largest of the numerous islands of the lake. In 1697 Peten was reduced by Don Martin Ursula, when making a highway from Campeché to Guatemala. The Spaniards do not appear to have occupied the district: It is now a province of Guatemala, but being geographically separated from the republic, has much greater intercourse with Yucatan and British Honduras. The Peteneros frequently visit Belize to buy and sell ; and a truck-road is now in process of construction from a point on the Old River to Peten, to encourage them, and develop further our trade with them in mules and cattle. The Peteneros are stout, swarthy, little folk, well-nurtured, and with a pleasing expression and gentle manners ; much given to balls, bull-fights, and " fiestas " generally.

It is said, in Stephen's " Incidents of Travel in Yucatan," that beyond the lake of Peten lies a wilderness, in which roam unknown tribes of Los Candones, or unbaptized Indians, and that in it there is a city never reached by a white man, but still occupied by wild Indians precisely in the same state they were before Columbus discovered America.

Mr. Stephens found traces of a superstition, the sign or symbol of which he discovered on the edifices of Yucatan—the "mano colorado" or red hand—the same symbol being in common use amongst certain tribes of North American Indians. The following specimen of the Maya language is from a translation into it of portions of Scripture by the Rev. Mr. Kingdon, a Baptist missionary of Belize. The last two verses of the Gospel of St. Matthew are here given :—

ɔocaán u binel cambizeex ti tulacalóob macóob taan u bulul leoob ti beti kaba ti leti Yum, iix ti leti takpal, iiv ti leti Espiritu Cilich. Taán u cambesic leoob u betáal tulacalóob leoob baalóob bicil teex yanhi tuxtic. Iix, ilac, ten yanen y teex tulacalóob kinóob tac leti xul ti noh hab. Tu hahil.

ɔ, as in *knats ;* c, always hard; a, as in *art ;* i, as in *me ;* x, sh ; k, ch with a strong clicking sound.[3]

Mosquito Indians.

The Mosquito Indians, or Waiknas, inhabiting the Shore, present marked differences from the interior tribes above-described. It is said they have a strong admixture of African blood in them, and although their features are regular, their hair has an undoubted curl in it. They are taller, and bony rather than muscular, their complexion ashy black, unlike the glossy hue of the Quiché race, or even the Carib..

[3] See Appendix B.

Their habits are nomadic almost—at all events unsettled—shifting their quarters with frequency. They live chiefly by fishing, and are dexterous in the management of their canoes. They hate Ladinos and Spanish-speaking Indians, and will assassinate them by stealth on an opportunity; but they are very fond of the English. They dislike being in houses when they come to Belize, and take possession of some private wharf or other, whose owner they have worked for. They are the most debased of all the aboriginal tribes of the region. Never having been subdued, they have retained their customs from early times, one of which is polygamy. There are traces of demon-worship among them, but no name even for the Deity. Their "Sukia" is a kind of fetish, or sorcerer, the servant of Walushu, the evil one. Their adoration of evil spirits arises from the original idea that they are likely to suffer more inconvenience from them than from beneficent powers. Their women are delicate and handsome, and are espoused at the early age of ten or twelve. When pregnant, a place is prepared for them in the depth of the woods, whence they are not allowed to emerge for a stated period. That accomplished, a public lustration of mother and infant takes place. Like all other Indians the Mosquito men are fond of rum. They are reputed to be addicted to crimes particularized in the first chapter of Romans.

The different tribes of Indians in Central America have each a dialect of their own, derived from one common stock, as European languages are from Sanskrit. Their work in red pottery and mat and basket-work cannot be excelled by savage tribes such as they are.

The Carib. The Caribs, although ubiquitous over the colony, are properly another coast tribe of mongrel breed and mixed descent. Although the Carib is found in the towns engaging in domestic service, on board lighters or coasting droghers "sailorizing," or away in the backwoods cutting logwood or mahogany, his proper element is the sea, coasting up and down in his mahogany, cedar, or "tubruse" creaw or dorey, bringing his yams and cassava to market. The principal Carib settlements are on such strips of sandy beach as are found to the southward at Stann Creek and Punta Gorda, Middle River and Red Cliff.

The Carib of Central America is not a pure Indian, but much more a descendant of Ham.

According to Bryan Edwardes, the original "Charaibe" was a warlike, tattooed cannibal, with an olive complexion, straight, black, coarse hair; "trained to draw the bow with unerring skill, wield the club with dexterity and strength, to swim with agility and boldness," and to fish. Such was the Red Carib of the islands, copper-coloured rather than olive-complexioned. The Carib of Central America is a woolly-headed, thick-lipped, ordinary-looking negro, showing little of the Indian strain in his physiognomy or the conformation of his skull; innocent of all acquaintance with bow and arrow or war-club or tattoo-marks, and also of cannibal propensities; but he can fish and sail or paddle a canoe, and is an amphibious creature, as much at home in as out of the water. He is a Christian where the Red Carib was an idolater, but he is, as his congener was, polygamous, superstitious, and migratory. Like the Carib of the islands, he will not eat peccary or turtle or manatee; he prefers salt fish and plantain, yams and pork, and cassava cakes. He has preserved a language which may or may not be traceable philologically to a true Carib source, but which, to hear a few of the people jabber it, sounds like nothing human. He manages to pick up Creole English well, and Spanish better, however. He is also found using the first twenty French numerals, and a few French words besides. The Scriptures in portions have been translated into Carib.[4]

Historically he is said to be descended from the Black Caribs of the Island of St. Vincent, on which island, somewhere about 1685, a ship from Guinea landed a cargo of Africans, intended as slaves for one of the other islands.

Accessions to these Africans were from time to time made of runaways from Barbados, and eventually a mixed race, in which the African element greatly predominated, sprang from intermixture. The Red Carib is only met with now-a-days in single instances, at very rare intervals. How the Black Carib was brought to Central America is an open question, but the spread of races in these regions is now very difficult to trace.[5] They have a system of authority amongst themselves, by which certain elders are obeyed as "captains." The Carib women are similar in physical outline to the

---

[4] Bryan Edwardes, "History of the West Indies."

[5] Crowe, page 48, states "that when partly exterminated by the British in St. Vincent, the remnant were finally expelled, 1796. Thence a residue were conveyed to Ruatan in men-of-war, and abandoned on that island, finding their way from Ruatan to the adjacent coasts, rapidly increasing in numbers, as they are still."

men. They are faithful, modest in demeanour, and, though given to a free display of well-developed personal charms, virtuous, except in the matter of polygamous connexions. Each wife has a hut for herself and progeny provided for her by her husband, whose scattered harem may be as extensive as his ability to build wigwams. Afterwards the wife supports herself in the plantation, planting and raising yams, manioc, poultry, and hogs, while the lordly husband goes fishing, or sailing to Belize, or reclines in his hammock. At times he will take service at a mahogany work or sugar rancho, or engage on board a coasting-vessel, but, although more inclined now to permanent labour than formerly, they are an unsettled race. They are likewise fond of rum and outbursts of festivity. The missionaries have greater success with Caribs than with the aboriginal Indians—with the Mosquito men little or none. The Carib has an inordinate share of vanity and frivolity, united to a fund of cheerful buoyancy of spirits, but he is limited as to intelligence and perseverance. They are quiet, inoffensive people, rather cowardly as a race, although in their canoes they will dare the roughest seas. They are subject to a peculiar skin disease, which is a description of leprosy, and shows in white spots on the hands and feet: the Creoles call those so marked "peckly Caribs," i.e. speckled Caribs. They construct very good huts of cane and posts, thatched with palm-leaves, roomy and lofty, and keep them neat and clean, and one of their settlements is an interesting spectacle of primitive domestic institutions, when one is not squeamish in the matter of how many establishments a paterfamilias may be allowed.

The mixed races of European and Indian descent, Mestizos. or Ladinos; Indian and African, or Sambos; and European and African, or Mulattos,—remain to be noticed.

The Ladinos—as the Mestizos of Central America and Mexico, the descendants of Spaniards and Indians, are designated in these localities—are a low-statured, fleshy race, light or dark in complexion according to the degree of admixture. The term Ladino signifies " gallant men," and, applied as it is, is quite a misnomer. They are by no means a brave race, and are very treacherous. They are intellectually, by cultivation, superior to the Indians, over whom they are a dominant class. Their habits are voluptuous, their moral tone low in the extreme. They are not so priest-ridden as the European Spaniards, but they have an inferior class of clergy to deal with—men who themselves are wanting in cultivation and moral excellence. The Sambos are limited in number—and amongst the Spanish-speaking inhabitants so also are the Mulattos ; the hidalgos of New Spain having preferred to mix the *sangre azul* with Indian rather than African blood—and partake of the habits and manners of their African or Indian progenitors according to circumstances. They have generally better and more regular features than Mulattos. The Mulattos—in which are included the various degrees of consanguinity described by the terms quadroon, octaroon, mustee, &c.—resemble in their most salient characteristics the products of slavery institutions everywhere. The coloured race—as distinct from the African or Creole African—have made some progress in social advancement and culture since abolition, without increasing in refinement or moral status. As has been mentioned previously, the slave of British Honduras never occupied the degraded position of the plantation slave. He was not driven in a gang to the drudgery of the field hoe under brutal overseers, but laboured side by side or under the eye of his owner, between whom and himself the best relations compatible with his condition of servitude existed. He lived the free life of the backwoods, wielding that noble tool, the axe, or the cutlass, and was kindly treated. The natural result is that to-day his descendants are in all respects superior to the coloured populations of other countries in which slavery once existed. He is more self-reliant, less crafty and cringing. A class of free people of colour sprang up early in the settlement's history, between whom and the handful of whites there never was drawn a hard and fast line of social distinction, such as was rigidly adhered to, and has not been removed yet, in places like Jamaica and Barbados.

The mahogany labourers of Honduras are capable of severe physical toil, less disinclined to undertake it, if they are not free from a common preference for intermittent industry, relieved by idle spells, and diversified by indulgence in feasting and merry-making. Intellectually the coloured race in the Islands are probably their superiors, morally there is a dead level, which is not a high one. They are as excitable as the race elsewhere, as frivolous and unreliable. Good-humoured, easily pleased, vain and passionate, but variable in all their humours and inconsequent in their ideas; insincere, and if not untruthful, given to exaggeration in their sentiments, and incapable, unassisted, of any organization. The labouring classes are much given to rum, music, dancing, and sexual pleasures. Their wants are easily supplied. Their dwellings are little better than out-houses, even in the towns; their food coarse and ill-prepared, consisting for the most part of salt fish, and plantains or yams, flour, pork, tropical fruits, vegetables, and fresh fish, with rice or cornflour; clothing light and inexpensive as a rule, although they spend a good portion of their wages on cheap finery and dressy but not costly clothes. They raise poultry and pigs, but buy nearly every other article of food. Tea they use little, but must have coffee, and consume large quantities of sugar in one form or another. They are healthy, as a rule, and active, but an epidemic of cholera or small-pox makes wholesale ravages among them. They are tolerably cleanly in their habits and persons.

In a great measure they are losing their respect for "Buckra," as it was once more generally their habit to call the white folks, and are becoming insolent, which they think is the same thing as being independent in manner. Their vanity and sensitiveness to slight or insult is sometimes amusing, and they "nurse their wrath to keep it warm," until in some shape they have obtained "satisfaction," as they say. A very deep insult is to allude to their progenitors, in a manner in the slightest degree derogatory. "Cuss me daddy, cuss me mammy," is to rouse their ire at once. Deprived of spectacular amusements, they elect the police-court as their house of the drama, and bring each other up before his worship on the slighest provoca-tion—indulging their self-importance, in default of a better platform, in the dock and witness-table alter-nately. Thus the time of the officials of the court is principally taken up listening to the choice Billingsgate interchanged between Miss Cudjoe and Mrs. Quashee, and in determining how much the latter must contribute to the revenue, in the shape of fines and costs, for her indulgence in abusive language familiarly known to them as "cussin."

There is considerable humour and practical wisdom embodied in some of their quaint sayings well expressed in their idiomatic Creole English.

"You heah massa caal you?" said one darkie to another, whom he was endeavouring to arouse. "Sleep no hab massa," replied the sluggard, rolling over on his other side to "slumber again." "Cry cry picney nebba hab right!" they apply to a querulous grum-bler, and they convert our proverb that all so-and-so's geese are swans into " Ebery John Crow tink um picney white," the young of the John Crow (*vultur aura*), the scavenger of these parts, being born with a fine cover-ing of white down, although the bird is ashy black at maturity. Again, their own proverb "Rock (s)tone bottom ob him ribba no feel de sun," is a recommenda-tion to humility in selecting one's position in life as ensuring immunity from the effects of the noonday heat of passion.

The Creoles of Belize are much less superstitious than the coloured populations of the islands. The

Obeah art is not unknown, or altogether without its practitioners and believers, but it has little hold even on the lowest classses.

The manner and morals of the " Baymen " in former times had doubtless a smack of the backwoods, with a flavour of the rollicking freedom of sea-life about them. They retained a dash of the original buccaneering element. They worked hard, and drank hard when they assembled on the coast to ship their wood. One is hardly disposed to moralize too gravely over Jack Tar enjoying his spree on shore after a long voyage, and when after nine months of toil and exposure in the bush, the Honduras wood-cutters met together at St. George's Caye or at Belize, we must not condemn too loudly their annual orgie. They lived a rough life, cut off from civilization and refining recreation, and as the pioneers of a lucrative trade cannot be judged by ordinary standards. They were honourable in their dealings, united amongst themselves, unbounded in their hospitable generosity to strangers, and, to their credit be it said, they lessened for their bondsmen the hardships of the lot of slavery.

But slavery here, as elsewhere, developed the same social taint which, as an institution, has marked its existence in every country it has cursed. Nor has that taint—laxity of morals—been eradicated from the blood of the descendants of the Baymen. It is only fair to say that no exalted standard of morals has ever been set up in the Bay, and that Europeans whom circumstances have made sojourners there have seldom presented the inhabitants with a pattern of purer

The Baymen and their descendants.

morality, while the communities around them were sunk in depravity with few redeeming traits.

Intellectual culture is almost unknown, and education of the primary sort even in a backward condition. Increased communication with more advanced countries, and the influx of a better class of permanent residents, it is hoped will work reformation and lead to social advancement. This much may be said, that there is always hope for a community which throws no cloak over its blemishes and sores, in which depravity assumes no sanctified mask, but in which the evil floats to the top like scum.

The white population is very limited and out of all proportions. Few white people but look upon it as a resting, not an abiding place, one from which they hope eventually to return enriched to their native soil. This, in more ways than one, is disadvantageous, but the day will surely come when a permanent upper class, refined and intellectually on a par with other countries, will form itself in Honduras; the tone of public morals will be elevated; more wholesome recreation provided for all classes, educational schemes promoted, and something over and above mere material prosperity looked upon as the chief end of existence.

CHAPTER XIV.

THE LABOUR QUESTION—CLIMATE—PRODUCTIONS—FLORA AND FAUNA—AND GENERAL FEATURES.

IN view of increased agricultural operations, conse- Labour
quent upon the anticipated extension of the cultivation Question.
of sugar, the development of the incipient fruit trade,
and the contingent demands for labour that these and
existing industries must give rise to, the question of
a supply of efficient labourers must soon press its
importance upon all connected with the colony, as
private members of the community, or as officials controlling its affairs.

The invincible distaste of the mass of native coloured
labourers to the avocations connected with the cultivation of the soil, and their inherent preference for
the life of the mahogany or logwood works, or of the
coasting-vessel, will necessitate agricultural capitalists
looking beyond the limits of the colony for plantation hands. At the same time, as it is certain that
agriculture will only supplement, not supplant, the older
staple industry of wood-cutting and shipping, it is by
no means desirable that a single labourer—or, for that
matter, a single pound of capital—should be withdrawn
from it to be diverted to the work of the sugar-estate
or the farm.

Chinese and Indian coolie immigration, to the extent to which it has been tried, has not apparently found favour in the eyes of employers. From the islands only the refuse of their labour-market finds its way to Honduras. The restless Carib is too migratory in his habits, although an excellent workman, to settle down permanently to the labour of cultivation. It is a drudgery he leaves to his women—he will wield the axe, the paddle, but the hoe he dislikes as much as does the Creole.

The indigenous Indian from beyond the limits might be made available to some extent could he be induced to quit his scattered village-homes, and this is perhaps the cheapest labour to be procured. Free immigration from Africa has been proposed, but as yet no feasible scheme, adequate to meet future wants, has been sufficiently ventilated. The general law that labour follows capital will probably operate here as elsewhere.

Truck
system.

The existence of a most pernicious system—long abolished in England—called the truck system, of settling with the labourers on wood-cutting establishments has been the bane of the colony. The first principle in this system, which exercises perhaps the most baneful influence on the labouring population, is the advance of three or more months' wages at the time of hiring. The labourer engages himself some time during the Christmas holidays for the ensuing year at say nine dollars per month. But he has just entered upon, or is in the height of, his few weeks' annual festivity, and he and the woman he lives with, and the children, if any, require money " to keep Christmas." He applies for, and is granted four months' advance of wages; probably taking three to begin with, and spending it out, returning for another month's advance. But by his agreement he is bound to take half of his wages in goods from his employer, who keeps in his store a stock of such goods as his hands require, and of a certainly inferior quality. First of all there is an undue advantage on the employer's side, allowing that the majority of employers are contented with nothing beyond legitimate percentages of profit. But even in extreme cases, where less conscientious employers are not over tender in conscience, the evil of his purchasing in the dearest market, instead of being allowed to take his money where he likes, is the lesser one only; the greater is that he receives these goods and the cash in the middle of a saturnalia of dissipation, and the consequences are the hard cash disappears like butter before the sun, finding its way into the tills of the rum-sellers. The goods are next sold at one half what he is charged for them; that money, or the greater part of it, also disappears, and another advance follows. The labourer has therefore to start his year's engagement three, four, or even five months in debt. On the works the same rule of half goods half cash is pursued, but he sees no more cash although he gets goods. The book-keeper of the gang keeps his account, debiting so much for every day he is absent from work, even from sickness, and exacting fines rigorously, the contract being in every way a tight one for the labourer. It is hardly necessary to add that when his season's work is over he finds himself in debt when he comes down to Belize for his Christmas spree. At no time is he capable of under-

standing his accounts clearly, and the time chosen for
settling his year's accounts is when he is enjoying
a continuous carousal, during which his small amount
of brains is further muddled by drink. It may be
admitted that there are employers who are rigidly
conscientious, but the system is a most pernicious one
in every way. The remedy is to abolish advances
altogether, and to pay each labourer his weekly wages
in cash, and let him buy his goods where he likes,
giving him, of course, his rations as now. Get rid
also of the Christmas carnival by destroying Belize
centralization for rioting and dissipation annually, and
establish the labourers near their work, with depôts on
the estate at which they may make their purchases.
Employers and employed will be eventually benefited
by the change, the former far above the petty and
inglorious gains of this detestable truck system with
its demoralizing influences.

Climate. Although lying within the tropics, the climate of
British Honduras is sub-tropical rather than tropical.
That is principally owing to the prevalence of easterly
trade-winds during four-fifths of the year, which when
they veer round to E.N.E. have a touch of rigour
in them by no means pleasant to the natives, or those
Europeans who have resided any length of time in
warm countries. On the other hand some natural
barrier or shield, such as high or mountain ranges to
the rear, would seem to protect the strip of coast
from the hot, miasma-laden breeze crossing the western
interior.

British Honduras has suffered the prolonged and
unmerited injustice of having been given a very bad

name for unhealthiness. " Fever-pot," " mud-bank," are specimens of the milder class of epithets applied to it by ennuyé military subs and other transitory residents, with a great deal more absence of truth than generally attaches to such inconsiderately-chosen epigrammatic distinctions. Military medical men, mindful of the necessity of making out a case for "extra climate pay," have not forgotten to dwell exhaustively on the swampy nature of the soil, and the climatic influences they supposed were exercised on the health of the troops by residence in the colony, their knowledge of the country being mostly limited to the marshes behind Newtown Barracks, and occasional trips in the commissariat pinnace to adjacent cayes. But, says more scientifically and conscientiously one of themselves in the medical report for 1879, " contrary to what might be expected from the swampy nature, slight elevation, and luxuriant vegetation of the country in the immediate vicinity of Belize, the climate is, on the whole, healthy," while the public medical officer, Dr. Hunter, completely refutes the' charge of insalubrity after an extended residence in that position in the colony. Five years' careful observations lead him to state the temperature as follows :—min. 78°; max. 82°; mean 80°. A table of meteorological statistics for the year 1878, and other information, appended to this volume, will show more conclusively than a long dissertation the nature of the climate and kind of weather prevalent. The rainfalls for the months of October and November of the year 1878 are abnormal.

The death-rate returns, the longevity of the people,

and the statistics of disease will contrast favourably, not with those of other tropical climates only, but with those of temperate regions. Belize enjoys almost perfect immunity from the epidemic visitations incident to the tropics, while endemic fever is limited to occasional sporadic cases, generally yielding to proper treatment. The yellow fever scourge has visited these shores, but never to commit the ravages it does in Jamaica, for example, or New Orleans. Small-pox does not commit greater havoc here than in Europe, and cholera merely pays a visit on its devastating march westward when all countries and climes suffer. more or less; there are no outbreaks of scarlatina or typhoid fever, and there is freedom from catarrh and bronchial affections, although influenza is prevalent during the " northers," wet and dry. The climate is particularly favourable in cases of phthisical complaints. The ailments of childhood are symptomatically milder, and yield more readily to treatment, and the small fry of all sizes and complexions are robust-looking and healthy.

The seasons here, as elsewhere in the tropics, naturally divide themselves into the wet and dry; but of the former there are two separate periods—a short "wet" in May or June of heavy showers, the proper wet season commencing in September and October, and lasting until February, during which there shall be few days of twenty-four hours unaccompanied by showers of rain, with variations of severe thunderstorms. Hurricanes are fortunately like angels' visits, few and far between, and there is no record of any injurious earthquake, although earth-rumblings are not uncommon. The inhabitants are dependent on the clouds for their supply of water for domestic purposes. It is stored in iron tanks and wooden vats, but excellent spring-water can be supplied by vessels proceeding for it to spots on the coast, and, at a pinch, water can be brought from some distance up the river. River-water, however, is less wholesome, and only used on an emergency, unless by the riverain population.

Europeans find exercise no exertion, and can even undergo a moderate amount of fatigue and exposure, as long as they avoid the fiercer rays of the noonday sun. The nights are generally cool and pleasant. Mosquitoes are bad, but as the Creole dialect says, "not too bad;" but during the prevalence of the breeze from certain quarters the swarms of sandflies render existence intolerable while these winds last. They rarely last any time, fortunately. In the bush the "doctor" —a handsomely-marked species of the order Diptera —and the Botlass fly inflict painful and pestilent bites on their victims, and cattle and silver ticks are the cause of numerous flesh-sores. A local leprous affection, called cacoabay, affects the hands, feet, and joints, and once established is most difficult to eradicate, but persons of cleanly habits are exempt from such diseases.

As the country becomes cleared and settled, a change will most likely take place in the climate, rainfall, and salubrity, and it must necessarily be one of improvement.

Having previously dealt with the principal woods, sugar, and rum, it is only necessary now to direct attention to the minor articles the region produces.

Minor Productions.

Coffee grows wild, and as the district of the higher lands of the south-west becomes opened up, this branch of production will probably receive attention. At present it is advocated that the description known as Liberian should be introduced for cultivation, as it does not insist on any particular altitude, but grows equally well near the sea,[1] and virgin forest is suitable to this variety.

Cacao. The cacao-tree also finds a kindly soil adapted to it, and there is every facility for establishing extensive walks of this handsome tree, productive of the most lucrative yields.

Tobacco. Tobacco of excellent quality is produced, and there are many spots in the district particularly suited to this plant. The leaf is dried and put up roughly for home consumption. Cigar manufacture has been recently attempted by Mr. C. T. Hunter, an enterprising merchant, and "weeds" for exportation, of a superior quality and make over the locally-consumed, ill-made specimens, are now shipped by him in large consignments, as well as an article furnished for the home-market at a reasonable price. This industry will undoubtedly form an important feature in the future commerce of the colony.

Cotton. Cotton has been experimented upon, and the results have received favourable mention, but the cultivation has not as yet been undertaken by experts in the raising and shipment of that staple. It is said that the shrub is liable to the attack of an insect fatal to its healthy growth.

Cochineal and sarsaparilla. Cochineal and sarsaparilla, as will be seen from

[1] Hooker.

returns already given, have long been amongst the minor articles of exportation and will always swell the returns of products.

Indigo and anatto are valuable dyes, which the country will yield extensively, and there are also medicinal plants indigenous to the soil, chinchona, jalap, aloes, copaiba, ipecacuanha, castor oil, and croton.

Indigo and anatto.

Grasses and fibres for mat and rope-making, paper-making, and other economical appliances, are numerously catalogued. The silk grass (*Agave sisilana*) is well known; an acre properly planted will yield three tons of this, the finest, toughest, largest-stapled fibre in the world. The ramie or China grass is stronger than the best flax or hemp; it requires less labour to cultivate than cotton, is not injured by worms or excess of rain. It is worth in England from 50*l.* to 80*l.* per ton. From the plantain and banana *stalks* beautiful fibrous material can be produced, and a coarser material from the cocoa-nut-tree and other palms.

Grasses and fibres.

There are several varieties of these—especially the red bean, much used as food by the Spanish Indian population and not neglected by the Creoles.

Leguminous plants.

The latter especially is extensively cultivated, but of course at present only for home use. The production of the former might be greatly increased, and the quality of the grain improved by more skilled farming.

Rice and maize.

Arrowroot and tapioca can be produced from the manioc or cassava, from which the Caribs now make starch and cassava bread for sale in the markets of Belize and elsewhere.

Arrowroot and tapioca.

Under this head may be catalogued nearly all the valuable West Indian spice-plants—pimento, mace and

Spices.

nutmeg (the former the reticulated scarlet arillus or outer covering enveloping the oval shell of the latter), and vanilla (an orchid).

Fruits and vege-tables. The pine-apple succeeds well, and the finest qualities of sugar-loaf and Spanish red are sold cheaply in the market. The citron family is represented in all its varieties—oranges, limes, lemons, forbidden fruit, and shaddock. The plantain forms the staple vegetable food of the community, and is now largely exported to New Orleans, its congener the banana accompanying it. Yams and other " ground provisions " abound, and to the fruits must be added the plentiful supply in season of mangoes, papaw, custard-apple, mammy-apple, monkey-cap, avocado-pear, melons, coco plum, and many others. Magnificent specimens of the bread-fruit-tree are to be seen loaded with fruit. But there remains the extensive family of palms, all of which are found here. The cabbage, with its smooth, perpendicular, columnar stem, is rather a graceful arboreal ornament than a useful production; and the excessive hardness of the cahoon-palm-nut renders the most powerful and expensive machinery necessary to express the valuable oil from it. Little description is necessary of the well-known cocoa-palm, its productions of fibre and nut are familiar to all. In 1880, 1,623,631 nuts were exported at prices averaging 18 dollars to 20 dollars per 1000.[2] It grows to advantage in the most sterile soils, along the sea shore of the coast and on the cayes, and there is almost no limit to the supply of the nut, which at present is almost entirely exported, husked, to America. The

[2] See Honduras Almanac.

valuable fibre is therefore not availed of, but could easily be prepared on the spot for European markets.

Magnificently is this country dowered with flowers Flowers. and flowering shrubs, the orchid family producing rare and valuable varieties, the glorious flamboyeau, the oleander, fragrant frangipanni, and countless specimens in the domain of Flora, delighting the eye and charming all the senses.

The woods abound in game and wild animals, the Fauna. small red deer, ten varieties of wild hog, the peccary (*Dicotyles labiatus*) and waree (a mere variety), the paca (*Cœlogenys subnigra*), a burrowing animal locally called gibbonet or gibnut, considered good eating; the coypus of the otter tribe, the glutton or wolverine, ant-eater, racoon, opossum, armadillo, and, amongst the aquatic mammals, the sea-cow or manatee; and the riverain, graminivorous, amphibious tapir.

The feline species is represented by the jaguar,[3] the puma,[4] tiger-cat,[5] &c., none of which are dangerous to man.

The agouti or Indian rabbit is also indigenous, and a specimen of the tribe of viverra, known locally as the quash, very useful in destroying vermin. Squirrels and foxes are numerous, the latter in the mountainous districts.

The quadrumana are confined to the sapajou and sagoin families, as the horned sapajou, apella, brown sapajou, capucin, &c.

Parrots of the red mangrove species fly in flocks, Birds and and the more valuable and talkative yellow-heads are reptiles. procured from the interior. Magnificent-plumaged

[3] F. onca.   [4] F. concolor.   [5] F. catus ferus.

cardinals, banana-birds (orioles), toucans, rice-birds, kingfishers and yellow-tails, fly about, with rare species unnamed, awaiting classification by the ornithologist. Raptorial birds—eagles, hawks, ospreys, vultures (especially the vultur aura)—are well represented. Of the gradiatorials there are pelicans, galdings, curlew, snipe, teal, herons, and others. The Honduras wild turkey has rather the plumage of the peacock than the turkey family, but it is now very rare; the curassow and crested curassow are common, also the quam (*Penelope cristata*).

Insects have been already alluded to. Centipedes are more common than scorpions. The lepidoptera are almost all present, and some huge specimens are seen flying in the interior. The coleoptera are principally represented by the chafers, longicorn and lamellicorn beetles, the tribe curculio and families of the elateridæ, lampyridæ, and coccinellidæ.

Ants. Ants and spiders are very numerous, and of various species.

Saurians. Alligators of enormous size infest the rivers, and the lizard family are numerous individually and specifically. The iguana and its eggs are considered great delicacies by some portions of the people. Few Europeans can be induced to partake of this food.

Chelonia. Turtle are shipped to Europe and America, and are plentifully found. Turtle-fishing employs a percentage of the population. There are three kinds—the green, used for food, the hawksbill, and loggerhead, caught for the shell, a valuable article of export. Land, or rather river tortoises—the terrapin, called here hecatee —of delicious flavour, find their way to market.

Serpents are in this region but too common, and some
are very deadly. The coral, barber's pole, jumping
tomagoff, rattlesnake, with numerous others, infest
the bush. The natives, English and Spanish, have
remedies of their own.

The crustacea of the terrestrial division are represented by the land or mountain-crab, an animal whose
habits require some description. According to Du
Testre, they live in orderly societies in holes in the
ground. In April or May they begin a migratory
march to the sea, taking a geometrically straight line,
and cover the land, marching at night over all intervening obstacles ; when, arrived at the coast, they spawn
and hatch their eggs in the sand, and after a time the
old ones march back with millions of their progeny to
the mountains. In August they fatten, when they are
eaten ; they then prepare to moult, and remain inactive
until the old shell is cast. In Jamaica the black
mountain-crab is considered *bonne-bouche.*

The seas of this region abound in fish of all description—baracouta, shark, king and Jew fish, bass,
mullet, snapper, sheephead, grouper, catfish, tarpaum,
mackerel, and the famous callipiver, the salmon of the
West Indians, a species of mullet. *Shell-fish :* the
stone-crab, crayfish, whelk, and lobster. Oysters of a
small breed are found sticking on the branches of the
marine shrub, the mangrove.

A small breed of horses, suitable for the country, is
maintained. Mules of excellent qualities are to be
purchased ; the ass is used here only for stud purposes. The usual friends of man, the cat and dog,
are present.

Minerals.   Gold-bearing quartz has been found. The mineral deposits are unexplored, but probably would repay exploration. More than one exploring expedition has been set on foot with varying results. Two American gentlemen in 1872, Colonel W. T. Mechlin and W. R. Warren, Esq., made a journey from Belize to the city of Guatemala, *viâ* Peten, Sacluc, and Coban, and their joint report has been printed. It has greater reference to Guatemala than Honduras, and directs attention chiefly to future means of communication between Belize and that republic, and recommends a railroad as a means of diverting trade at present carried on by the Pacific to Belize. "All that benefits Guatemala," it says, "would equally assist Belize." In 1878 another movement was set on foot to explore the unknown parts of the colony, partly under government, partly under private auspices : Messrs. Drake and Worth, the former a sugar-planter who is also an old traveller and explorer, the latter a miner who had recently arrived in Belize. They ascended the Cockscombs to an elevation of 2000 feet. They were away a month, but found the difficulties of their project greater than they had anticipated, and returned without effecting much. Great disappointment was felt, and as their resources were still unexhausted, another expedition was resolved on, and they started again, accompanied by the present colonial secretary, and depending on Indians for packers left Belize in a pitpan on the 23rd of November, 1878, for the Cay (Old River), so far following the route of Mechlin and Warren. They returned to Belize on the 18th of January, 1879. We

(marginal notes:) Minerals. Explorations for Minerals.

refer to the report itself (published at the government printing-office) for details, merely extracting the following summary of results by Mr. Fowler (page 35).

" The result of the expedition may be briefly summed up as follows :—The interior of the colony was found to be a succession of valleys and hills from 1200 feet to 3300 feet above the level of the sea, and may be divided into pastoral, mineral, and agricultural districts, each of which can be fairly defined. The most important discovery to be considered is the indications of mineral wealth. The sandstone, shale, anthracite, quartz, and veins of ores met with, together with the formation of the country, justify the belief that it is highly probable coal, gold, and silver may be found. This mineral district is a belt of country twenty or thirty miles broad, running north-east and south-west from the south of the Cockscomb range into the neighbouring republics of Guatemala and Honduras, and parallel to and distant from the coast, as the crow flies, about twenty-five miles. It is known that opals and gold have been found, and gold-mines are being worked in these countries which adjoin our frontier. The quantity of gold-dust produced from the Honduras mines has increased considerably of late, and it has become a means of remittance in consequence of currency difficulties. I ascertained that 1756 ounces have been shipped from Belize during the past six months, which have been obtained immediately south of us. I have lately seen nuggets from Honduras weighing over three ounces, &c."

CHAPTER XV.

CONCLUSION.

A REGION of upwards of six thousand square miles, or four million acres in area, four-fifths of which consists of rich arable lands laid down in virgin alluvial soil capable of producing in abundance the commodities demanded by the requirements of more civilized countries and populous communities; whose boundless forest tracts will yet yield unlimited supplies of massive logs of costly timber and valuable dye-woods; whose mineral resources, as yet untouched, there is warrant for saying are very extensive; whose plateaux and mountain altitudes are adapted to specific culti-vation; whose cayes and sea-beach, so far from being mere sandy wastes, will become remunerative cocoa-nut walks; whose swampiest portions can be made available for the growth of such congenial plants as tobacco—lies waiting the advent of fresh energy and increased capital. The more elevated districts of the interior are extensive pasture-land for stock-raising; the slopes of the adjacent hills are well adapted to coffee and cacao-trees; the waters surrounding its coasts teem with myriads of the finny tribe of delicious flavour; its forests abound in game; and, without trenching on other industries of cultivation, there is more than a sufficiency of land for vegetable culture for the supply of four times the existing population. But the question of food-supply is further rendered easy by its contiguity to the open ports of the New World, which are communicated with by steam in a few days.

The present population is numerically inadequate to the development of such a region, and as yet no sufficiently alluring scheme of immigration has been inaugurated, or even under consideration, to induce the right stamp of settlers to select it as their home. An agricultural labouring class has yet to be formed, and considerable augmentation of the class of moneyed planters is desiderated.

The system of monopoly, which allowed a few wealthy firms connected with its timber trade to cramp the development of the colony generally by the hold they had acquired over large tracts of land, has been in a great measure broken up by the failure of some of those who followed a dog-in-the-manger policy, and the awakening of others to the truth that their real and permanent interests are bound up in the general advancement, and not confined to selfish ends only. There is little danger of that system re-establishing itself to press down the colony under its weight like another Old Man of the Sea.

The accommodating waterways of the region will always be found useful, but internal communication by road and rail is necessary to open up the country away from the coast and river-banks. The harbours along its coast-line are capable of improvement, and

its coasting trade of reform and extension. But con-
jointly with these improvements the main objects
ought to be "to tap the back regions."

But the suicidal step taken by the local legislature
in 1869-70 must be reversed in view of the future of
the colony.

The evil of irresponsible power, in the form of a
crown colony government, which leaves the interests
of all in the hands of one man, selected often without
due qualifications for the exercise of such unlimited
authority by the Colonial Office, are even now palpably
felt, and keenly so, by the inhabitants who were betrayed by their former representatives voting away
the constitution.

It is an anachronism in the history of the British
Empire, an anomaly in the existing state of its political institutions, that such despotic rule as that of
crown colony government is present in any portion
of the dominions of a constitutional sovereign; that
any fragment of that empire peopled by free-born
British subjects, over which floats the flag of free
England, should be deprived of representative government, and its population of the control of their own
finances. Such a state of affairs can no longer be
allowed to continue without—on each occasion when
the demands of the colonists for restitution of self-
government are refused—discredit and a valid charge of
infidelity to the principles of political freedom being
brought against the successive administrations declining to grant restoration of free institutions to the
colony.

The colony in question is surrounded on every side

by free republics, the offspring of priest-ridden, monarchical Spain, all boasting of possessing the ines-
timable privileges of representation and responsible
government, and in the region where it is situate the
only single spot destitute of free institutions upon
which the finger can be placed in the map is the
British Colony of Honduras!

It is not because a colony has been contented and
law-abiding throughout its history that advantage
should be taken of it.

It were a more a graceful act to restore its privileges now, than to postpone the reversion to the former
free constitution until its voice becomes so powerful
that a deaf ear can no longer be turned to its demands.

No definite improvements will ever be carried out
under this system; for what one lieutenant-governor,
absolute for five years, does, his successor will not
continue, or will undo. There has been no social
amelioration or educational advancement, and no continuous effort to encourage even material progress
under the "paternal system."

True, the trade and commerce of the country, displaying unusual vitality and energy, have forced themselves forward in spite of obstacles, the mistaken policies
of diverse executives, and short-sighted, selfish monopolists, and the neglect of home authorities, whose ideas
are limited by their geographical acquirements—many
of them not being sure whether Honduras is an island
in the West Indian group, a mountain in Mexico, or
a part of the South American continent!

If in laying this retrospect of the past career of the

colony before the public, the compiler has even in a slight measure smoothed the path of progress, or given that progress of the colony ever so gentle an impulse by turning attention to it, he will be more than sufficiently rewarded for the not inconsiderable labour of research and compilation which he has now completed.

APPENDIX A.

Meteorological Observations during 1878, at Belize.

Month	Barometer Reading			Temperature of Air					Mean of		Rainfall		Wind	Remarks
	Mean	Maximum	Minimum	Maximum	Minimum	Mean of Maximum	Mean of Minimum	Mean Daily Range	Dry Bulb	Wet Bulb	No. of days	Collection; inches	General Directions	
January	29·51	30·08	29·50	90·00	78·00	86·98	69·25	17·13	85·76	78·41	12	4·29	N. & N.W.	Cool; westerly winds; occasional showers.
February ...	30·03	30·91	29·91	86·00	65·00	82·01	73·19	8·82	79·56	76·67	1	1·50	S.E. & N.	Northerly winds; dry, cool, and pleasant.
March	30·13	30·08	29·34	89·25	68·00	84·70	79·80	4·00	83·81	83·91	4	2·16	S.E. & N.W.	Warm and dry; showers at night.
April.........	29·91	29·97	29·15	92·00	80·00	88·00	82·00	6·00	87·47	87·47	2	·50	S.E.E.	Dry with few hot days.
May	29·08	30·09	29·01	89·50	75·60	87·00	81·28	5·72	86·60	86·66	12	3·85	"	Sultry; occasional showers.
June	29·90	30·10	29·02	89·00	72·25	87·45	79·62	8·83	87·02	87·02	10	6·40	S.E.E.	Fine and pleasant.
July	30·00	30·01	29·84	88·75	75·00	86·97	81·27	5·70	86·27	86·27	16	4·41	S.E.	Generally dry; squalls.
August	29·99	30·01	29·84	80·25	75·00	87·41	80·45	6·90	86·50	86·50	18	5·61	"	Much lightning, thunder, and rain.
September...	29·03	30·04	29·88	89·50	72·25	86·54	77·04	9·50	84·45	84·45	20	20·00	N.N.W.	Heavy rain and thunder storms.
October......	29·96	30·03	29·79	88·75	70·00	84·12	75·28	8·84	74·52	74·52	21	29·80	"	Largest rainfall yet recorded on 19th.
November...	30·01	30·13	29·93	84·25	64·50	80·72	71·83	8·89	78·82	78·82	16	15·79	N.W. & N.E.	Cold, dull, heavy rains.
December...	29·90	30·13	29·23	81·50	61·00	77·75	64·71	13·04	76·70	76·70	16	10·41	N.	Lowest temperature; greatest variation of thermometer; rain.

RAINFALL AT BELIZE, BRITISH HONDURAS, FOR THE
YEARS FOLLOWING.

	1863.	1864.	1865.	1866.	1867.	1869.	Total in six years.	Mean of six years.
Total . .	54·12	77·87	71·67	67·40	68·84	60	420	70
Average per month.	4·51	6·49	5·99	5·62	7·40	5	35	...

HEIGHTS (OLD RIVER POINTS) FROM BAROMETRICAL
OBSERVATIONS.

Point.	Sea-level to river-level.		Sea-level to top of bank.		River-level to top of bank.		From Belize.
	ft.	in.	ft.	in.	ft.	in.	Miles.[1]
Orange Walk	32	0	60	0	28	0	40
Young Girl Bank	34	6	68	10	34	0	45
Mount Hope	172	3	207	10	35	7	50
Spanish Look-Out.........	172	8	207	0	34	0	55
Duck Run	173	0	242	0	69	2	58

[1] As the crow flies.

APPENDIX B.

EXTRACTS FROM THE POPUL VUH, OR SACRED BOOK OF THE QUICHÉ INDIANS OF CENTRAL AMERICA.

(See Professor J. G. Dawsons's " Origin of the World," p. 22: Dawson Brothers, Montreal, 1877.)

Professor Dawson, in giving the following extracts from the Quiché Bible or sacred writings, says it is " an undoubted product of prehistoric religion in the Western Continent." He says also in a note that he avails himself of the condemned translation in Bancroft's " Native Races," vol. iii. " The original French translation of Brasseur du Bourbourg is more full."

EXTRACTS.

" And the heaven was formed, and all the signs thereof set in their angle and alignment, and its boundaries fixed towards the four winds by the Creator and Former and Mother and Father of life and existence—he by whom all move and breathe, the Father and Cherisher of the peace of nations and of the civilization of his people—he whose wisdom has perfected the excellence of all that is on the earth, or in the lakes, or in the sea.

" Behold the first word and the first discourse. There was yet no man, nor any animal . . . nothing was but the firmament. The face of the earth had not yet appeared over the peaceful

sea, and all the space of the heaven . . . nothing but immobility
and silence in the night.

" Alone also the Creator, the Former, the Dominator, the
Feathered Serpent—those that engender, those that give béing
—they are upon the water like a growing light. They are
enveloped in green and blue, and therefore their name is
Gucumatz.[1]

" Lo ! now the heavens exist, now exists also the Heart of
Heaven ; such is the name of God. It is thus he is called.
And they spake ; they consulted together and meditated ; they
mingled their words and their opinions.

" And the creation [of the earth] was verily after this wise.
Earth, they said, and on the instant it was formed ; like a
cloud or a fog was its beginning. Then the mountains and the
plains were visible, and the cypress and the pine appeared.
Then were the Gucumatz filled with joy, crying out, Blessed|be
thy coming, O Heart of Heaven, Thunderbolt. Our work and
our labour has accomplished its end."

" This corresponds," says the learned professor, " to the first
four creative days ; and next details are given as to the introduction of animals, with which, however, the Creator is dissatisfied, because they could not know or invoke the Creator.
Then comes the creation of man, also imperfect, for he has
speech without intelligence : so he is destroyed by water ; after
which a new race of man is produced of which it is related,
' they forgot the Heart of Heaven.' These were partly destroyed
by fire, a part turned into apes. Lastly, the perfect race of
man was formed, and the book goes on with the early history
and migrations of men."

Similar traditions, whose connexion with ancient Semitic
and Turanian revelations in Asia is unquestionable, existed
among the aboriginal Mexicans and Indian tribes of America
in ruder forms.

[1] The Feathered Serpent is perhaps the representative of the
Dragon and Serpent in the Semitic version ; but has not the same
evil import, and his colour gave sacredness to blue and green stones,
as the turquoise and emerald, both in North and South America, and
perhaps also in Asia and Africa.

LONDON
PRINTED BY GILBERT AND RIVINGTON, LIMITED,
ST. JOHN'S SQUARE.

A Catalogue of American and Foreign Books Published or Imported by MESSRS. SAMPSON LOW & CO. *can be had on application.*

Crown Buildings, 188, Fleet Street, London, November, 1882.

𝔄 𝔖𝔢𝔩𝔢𝔠𝔱𝔦𝔬𝔫 𝔣𝔯𝔬𝔪 𝔱𝔥𝔢 𝔏𝔦𝔰𝔱 𝔬𝔣 𝔅𝔬𝔬𝔨𝔰

PUBLISHED BY

SAMPSON LOW, MARSTON, SEARLE, & RIVINGTON.

ALPHABETICAL LIST.

A CLASSIFIED Educational Catalogue of Works published in Great Britain. Demy 8vo, cloth extra. Second Edition, revised and corrected, 5s.

About Some Fellows. By an ETON BOY, Author of "A Day of my Life." Cloth limp, square 16mo, 2s 6d.

Adams (C. K.) Manual of Historical Literature. Crown 8vo, 12s. 6d.

Adventures of a Young Naturalist. By LUCIEN BIART, with 117 beautiful Illustrations on Wood. Edited and adapted by PARKER GILLMORE. Post 8vo, cloth extra, gilt edges, New Edition, 7s. 6d.

Alcott (Louisa M.) Jimmy's Cruise in the "Pinafore." With 9 Illustrations. Second Edition. Small post 8vo, cloth gilt, 3s. 6d.

—————— *Aunt Jo's Scrap-Bag.* Square 16mo, 2s. 6d. (Rose Library, 1s.)

—————— *Little Men: Life at Plumfield with Jo's Boys.* Small post 8vo, cloth, gilt edges, 3s. 6d. (Rose Library, Double vol. 2s.)

—————— *Little Women.* 1 vol., cloth, gilt edges, 3s. 6d. (Rose Library, 2 vols., 1s. each.)

—————— *Old-Fashioned Girl.* Best Edition, small post 8vo, cloth extra, gilt edges, 3s. 6d. (Rose Library, 2s.)

—————— *Work, and Beginning Again.* A Story of Experience. (Rose Library, 2 vols., 1s. each.)

—————— *Shawl Straps.* Small post 8vo, cloth extra, gilt, 3s. 6d.

—————— *Eight Cousins; or, the Aunt Hill.* Small post 8vo, with Illustrations, 3s. 6d.

—————— *The Rose in Bloom.* Small post 8vo, 3s. 6d.

—————— *Under the Lilacs.* Small post 8vo, cloth extra, 5s.

A

Alcott (*Louisa M.*) *An Old-Fashioned Thanksgiving Day.* Small post 8vo, 3s. 6d.

—— *Proverbs.* Small post 8vo, 3s. 6d.

—— *Jack and Jill.* Small post 8vo, cloth extra, 5s.
"Miss Alcott's stories are thoroughly healthy, full of racy fun and humour . . . exceedingly entertaining . . . . We can recommend the 'Eight Cousins.'"—*Athenæum.*

Aldrich (*T. B.*) *Friar Jerome's Beautiful Book, &c.* Very choicely printed on hand-made paper, parchment cover, 3s. 6d.

—— *Poetical Works. Édition de Luxe.* Very handsomely bound and illustrated, 21s.

Alford (*Lady Marian*) See "Embroidery."

Allen (*E. A.*) *Rock me to Sleep, Mother.* 18 full-page Illustrations, elegantly bound, fcap. 4to, 5s.

American Men of Letters. Lives of Thoreau, Irving, Webster. Small post 8vo, cloth, 2s. 6d. each.

Ancient Greek Female Costume. By J. MOYR SMITH. Crown 8vo, 112 full-page Plates and other Illustrations, 7s. 6d.

Andersen (*Hans Christian*) *Fairy Tales.* With 10 full-page Illustrations in Colours by E. V. B. Cheap Edition, 5s.

Andres (*E.*) *Fabrication of Volatile and Fat Varnishes,* Lacquers, Siccatives, and Sealing Waxes. 8vo, 12s. 6d.

Angling Literature in England ; and Descriptions of Fishing by the Ancients. By O. LAMBERT. With a Notice of some Books on other Piscatorial Subjects. Fcap. 8vo, vellum, top gilt, 3s. 6d.

Archer (*William*) *English Dramatists of To-day.* Crown 8vo, 8s. 6d.

Arnold (*G. M.*) *Robert Pocock, the Gravesend Historian.* Crown 8vo, cloth. [*In the Press.*

Art and Archæology (*Dictionary*). See "Illustrated."

Art Education. See "Illustrated Text Books," "Illustrated Dictionary," "Biographies of Great Artists."

Art Workmanship in Gold and Silver. Large 8vo, 2s. 6d.

Art Workmanship in Porcelain. Large 8vo, 2s. 6d.

Artists, Great. See "Biographies."

Audsley (*G. A.*) *Ornamental Arts of Japan.* 90 Plates, 74 in Colours and Gold, with General and Descriptive Text. 2 vols., folio, £16 16s.

Audsley (*W. and G. A.*) *Outlines of Ornament.* Small folio, very numerous Illustrations, 31s. 6d.

Auerbach (*B.*) *Spinoza.* 2 vols., 18mo, 4s.

Autumnal Leaves. By F. G. HEATH. Illustrated by 12 Plates, exquisitely coloured after Nature; 4 Page and 14 Vignette Drawings. Cloth, imperial 16mo, gilt edges, 14*s.*

BANCROFT (G.) History of the Constitution of the United States of America. 2 vols., 8vo, 24*s.*

Barrett. English Church Composers. Crown 8vo, 3*s.*

THE BAYARD SERIES.
Edited by the late J. HAIN FRISWELL.

Comprising Pleasure Books of Literature produced in the Choicest Style as Companionable Volumes at Home and Abroad.

"We can hardly imagine better books for boys to read or for men to ponder over."—*Times.*

Price 2s. 6d. each Volume, complete in itself, flexible cloth extra, gilt edges, with silk Headbands and Registers.

The Story of the Chevalier Bayard. By M. De Berville.

De Joinville's St. Louis, King of France.

The Essays of Abraham Cowley, including all his Prose Works.

Abdallah; or, The Four Leaves. By Edouard Laboullaye.

Table-Talk and Opinions of Napoleon Buonaparte.

Vathek: An Oriental Romance. By William Beckford.

The King and the Commons. A Selection of Cavalier and Puritan Songs. Edited by Professor Morley.

Words of Wellington: Maxims and Opinions of the Great Duke.

Dr. Johnson's Rasselas, Prince of Abyssinia. With Notes.

Hazlitt's Round Table. With Biographical Introduction.

The Religio Medici, Hydriotaphia, and the Letter to a Friend. By Sir Thomas Browne, Knt.

Ballad Poetry of the Affections. By Robert Buchanan.

Coleridge's Christabel, and other Imaginative Poems. With Preface by Algernon C. Swinburne.

Lord Chesterfield's Letters, Sentences, and Maxims. With Introduction by the Editor, and Essay on Chesterfield by M. de Ste.-Beuve, of the French Academy.

Essays in Mosaic. By Thos. Ballantyne.

My Uncle Toby; his Story and his Friends. Edited by P. Fitzgerald.

Reflections; or, Moral Sentences and Maxims of the Duke de la Rochefoucauld.

Socrates: Memoirs for English Readers from Xenophon's Memorabilia. By Edw. Levien.

Prince Albert's Golden Precepts.

A Case containing 12 Volumes, price 31s. 6d.; or the Case separately, price 3s. 6d.

Beaconsfield (Life of Lord). See "Hitchman."

Begum's Fortune (The): A New Story. By JULES VERNE. Translated by W. H. G. KINGSTON. Numerous Illustrations. Crown 8vo, cloth, gilt edges, 7*s.* 6*d.*; plainer binding, plain edges, 5*s.*

A 2

Ben Hur: A Tale of the Christ. By L. WALLACE. Crown 8vo, 6s.

Beumers' German Copybooks. In six gradations at 4d. each.

Bickersteth's Hymnal Companion to Book of Common Prayer may be had in various styles and bindings from 1d. to 21s. *Price List and Prospectus will be forwarded on application.*

Bickersteth (Rev. E. H., M.A.) The Clergyman in his Home. Small post 8vo, 1s.

——— *The Master's Home-Call; or, Brief Memorials of Alice* Frances Bickersteth. 20th Thousand. 32mo, cloth gilt, 1s.

——— *The Master's Will.* A Funeral Sermon preached on the Death of Mrs. S. Gurney Buxton. Sewn, 6d.; cloth gilt, 1s.

——— *The Shadow of the Rock.* A Selection of Religious Poetry. 18mo, cloth extra, 2s. 6d.

——— *The Shadowed Home and the Light Beyond.* 7th Edition, crown 8vo, cloth extra, 5s.

Biographies of the Great Artists (Illustrated). Crown 8vo, emblematical binding, 3s. 6d. per volume, except where the price is given.

Claude Lorrain.*
Correggio, by M. E. Heaton, 2s. 6d.
Della Robbia and Cellini, 2s. 6d.*
Albrecht Dürer, by R. F. Heath.
Figure Painters of Holland.
Fra Angelico, Masaccio, and Botticelli.
Fra Bartolommeo, Albertinelli, and Andrea del Sarto.
Gainsborough and Constable.
Ghiberti and Donatello, 2s. 6d.
Giotto, by Harry Quilter.
Hans Holbein, by Joseph Cundall.
Hogarth, by Austin Dobson.
Landseer, by F. G. Stevens.
Lawrence and Romney, by Lord Ronald Gower, 2s. 6d.
Leonardo da Vinci.
Little Masters of Germany, by W. B. Scott.

Mantegna and Francia.
Meissonier, by J. W. Mollett, 2s. 6d.
Michelangelo Buonarotti, by Clément.
Murillo, by Ellen E Minor, 2s. 6d.
Overbeck, by J. B. Atkinson.
Raphael, by N. D'Anvers.
Rembrandt, by J. W. Mollett.
Reynolds, by F. S. Pulling.
Rubens, by C. W. Kett.
Tintoretto, by W. R. Osler.
Titian, by R. F. Heath.
Turner, by Cosmo Monkhouse.
Vandyck and Hals, by P. R. Head.
Velasquez, by E. Stowe.
Vernet and Delaroche, by J. R. Rees.
Watteau, by J. W. Mollett, 2s. 6d.*
Wilkie, by J. W. Mollett.

* *Not yet published.*

Bird (H. E.) Chess Practice. 8vo, 2s. 6d.

Birthday Book. Extracts from the Writings of R. W. Emerson. Square 16mo, cloth extra, numerous Illustrations, very choice binding, 3s. 6d.

——— *Extracts from the Poems of Whittier.* Square 16mo, with numerous Illustrations and handsome binding, 3s. 6d.

Birthday Book. Extracts from the Writings of Thomas à Kempis. Large 16mo, red lines, 3*s.* 6*d.*

Black (Wm.) Three Feathers. Small post 8vo, cloth extra, 6*s.*

—— *Lady Silverdale's Sweetheart, and other Stories.* 1 vol., small post 8vo, 6*s.*

—— *Kilmeny: a Novel.* Small post 8vo, cloth, 6*s.*

—— *In Silk Attire.* 3rd Edition, small post 8vo, 6*s.*

—— *A Daughter of Heth.* 11th Edition, small post 8vo, 6*s.*

—— *Sunrise.* Small post 8vo, 6*s.*

Blackmore (R. D.) Lorna Doone. Small post 8vo, 6*s.*

—— *Édition de luxe.* Crown 4to, very numerous Illustrations, cloth, gilt edges, 31*s.* 6*d.*; parchment, uncut, top gilt, 35*s.*

—— *Alice Lorraine.* Small post 8vo, 6*s.*

—— *Clara Vaughan.* 6*s.*

—— *Cradock Nowell.* New Edition, 6*s.*

—— *Cripps the Carrier.* 3rd Edition, small post 8vo, 6*s.*

—— *Mary Anerley.* New Edition, small post 8vo, 6*s.*

—— *Erema; or, My Father's Sin.* Small post 8vo, 6*s.*

—— *Christowell.* Small post 8vo, 6*s.*

Blossoms from the King's Garden: Sermons for Children. By the Rev. C. BOSANQUET. 2nd Edition, small post 8vo, cloth extra, 6*s.*

Bock (Carl). The Head Hunters of Borneo: Up the Mahakkam, and Down the Barita; also Journeyings in Sumatra. 1 vol., super-royal 8vo, 32 Coloured Plates, cloth extra, 36*s.*

Bonwick (James) First Twenty Years of Australia. Crown 8vo, 5*s.*

—— *Port Philip Settlement.* 8vo, numerous Illustrations, 21*s.*

Book of the Play. By DUTTON COOK. New and Revised Edition. 1 vol., cloth extra, 3*s.* 6*d.*

Bower (G. S.) Law relating to Electric Lighting. Crown 8vo, 5*s.*

Boy's Froissart (The). Selected from the Chronicles of England, France, and Spain. Illustrated, square crown 8vo, 7*s.* 6*d.* See " Froissart."

Boy's King Arthur (The). With very fine Illustrations. Square crown 8vo, cloth extra, gilt edges, 7*s.* 6*d.* Edited by SIDNEY LANIER, Editor of " The Boy's Froissart."

Boy's Mabinogion (The): being the Original Welsh Legends of King Arthur. Edited by SIDNEY LANIER. With numerous very graphic Illustrations. Crown 8vo, cloth, gilt edges, 7*s.* 6*d.*

Brassey (Lady) Tahiti. With Photos. by Colonel Stuart-Wortley. Fcap. 4to, 21*s.*

Breton Folk : An Artistic Tour in Brittany. By HENRY
BLACKBURN, Author of "Artists and Arabs," "Normandy Pictu-
resque," &c. With 171 Illustrations by RANDOLPH CALDECOTT.
Imperial 8vo, cloth extra, gilt edges, 21*s.*; plainer binding, 10*s. 6d.*

Bryant (W. C.) and Gay (S. H.) History of the United States.
4 vols., royal 8vo, profusely Illustrated, 60*s.*

Bryce (Prof.) Manitoba. Crown 8vo, 7*s. 6d.*

Burnaby (Capt.). See "On Horseback."

Burnham Beeches (Heath, F. G.). With numerous Illustrations
and a Map. Crown 8vo, cloth, gilt edges, 3*s. 6d.* Second Edition.

Butler (W. F.) The Great Lone Land ; an Account of the Red
River Expedition, 1869-70. With Illustrations and Map. Fifth and
Cheaper Edition, crown 8vo, cloth extra, 7*s. 6d.*

———— *Invasion of England, told twenty years after, by an Old*
Soldier. Crown 8vo, 2*s. 6d.*

———— *The Wild North Land ; the Story of a Winter Journey*
with Dogs across Northern North America. Demy 8vo, cloth, with
numerous Woodcuts and a Map, 4th Edition, 18*s.* Cr. 8vo, 7*s. 6d.*

———— *Red Cloud ; or, the Solitary Sioux.* Imperial 16mo,
numerous illustrations, gilt edges, 7*s. 6d.*

Buxton (H. J. W.) Painting, English and American. Crown
8vo, 5*s.*

CADOGAN (Lady A.) Illustrated Games of Patience.
Twenty-four Diagrams in Colours, with Descriptive Text. Foolscap
4to, cloth extra, gilt edges, 3rd Edition, 12*s. 6d.*

California. Illustrated, 12*s. 6d.* See "Nordhoff."

Cambridge Trifles ; or, Splutterings from an Undergraduate
Pen. By the Author of "A Day of my Life at Eton," &c. 16mo,
cloth extra, 2*s. 6d.*

Capello (H.) and Ivens (R.) From Benguella to the Territory
of Yacca. Translated by ALFRED ELWES. With Maps and over
130 full-page and text Engravings. 2 vols., 8vo, 42*s.*

Carlyle (T.) Reminiscences of my Irish Journey in 1849.
Crown 8vo, 7*s. 6d.*

Challamel (M. A.) History of Fashion in France. With 21
Plates, specially coloured by hand, satin-wood binding, imperial
8vo, 28*s.*

Changed Cross (The), and other Religious Poems. 16mo, 2*s. 6d.*

Child of the Cavern (The) ; or, Strange Doings Underground.
By JULES VERNE. Translated by W. H. G. KINGSTON. Numerous
Illustrations. Sq. cr. 8vo, gilt edges, 7*s. 6d.* ; cl., plain edges, 3*s. 6d.*

Choice Editions of Choice Books. 2s. 6d. each. Illustrated by
C. W. COPE, R.A., T. CRESWICK, R.A., E. DUNCAN, BIRKET
FOSTER, J. C. HORSLEY, A.R.A., G. HICKS, R. REDGRAVE, R.A.,
C. STONEHOUSE, F. TAYLER, G. THOMAS, H. J. TOWNSHEND,
E. H. WEHNERT, HARRISON WEIR, &c.

Bloomfield's Farmer's Boy.	Milton's L'Allegro.
Campbell's Pleasures of Hope.	Poetry of Nature. Harrison Weir.
Coleridge's Ancient Mariner.	Rogers' (Sam.) Pleasures of Memory.
Goldsmith's Deserted Village.	Shakespeare's Songs and Sonnets.
Goldsmith's Vicar of Wakefield.	Tennyson's May Queen.
Gray's Elegy in a Churchyard.	Elizabethan Poets.
Keat's Eve of St. Agnes.	Wordsworth's Pastoral Poems.

" Such works are a g.orious beatification for a poet."—*Athenæum.*

Christ in Song. By Dr. PHILIP SCHAFF. A New Edition,
revised, cloth, gilt edges, 6s.

Confessions of a Frivolous Girl (The): A Novel of Fashionable
Life. Edited by ROBERT GRANT. Crown 8vo, 6s. Paper boards, 1s.

Coote (W.) Wanderings South by East. Illustrated, 8vo, 21s.

Cornet of Horse (The): A Story for Boys. By G. A. HENTY.
Crown 8vo, cloth extra, gilt edges, numerous graphic Illustrations, 5s.

Cripps the Carrier. 3rd Edition, 6s. *See* BLACKMORE.

Cruise of H.M.S. " Challenger" (The). By W. J. J. SPRY, R.N.
With Route Map and many Illustrations. 6th Edition, demy 8vo, cloth,
18s. Cheap Edition, crown 8vo, some of the Illustrations, 7s. 6d.

Cruise of the Walnut Shell (The). An instructive and amusing
Story, told in Rhyme, for Children. With 32 Coloured Plates.
Square fancy boards, 5s.

D'ANVERS (N.) An Elementary History of Art. Crown
8vo, 10s. 6d.

—— *Elementary History of Music.* Crown 8vo, 2s. 6d.

Daughter (A) of Heth. By W. BLACK. Crown 8vo, 6s.

Day of My Life (A); or, Every-Day Experiences at Eton.
By an ETON BOY, Author of "About Some Fellows." 16mo, cloth
extra, 2s. 6d. 6th Thousand.

Decoration. Vol. II., folio, 6s. Vol. III., New Series, folio,
7s. 6d.

De Leon (E.) Egypt under its Khedives. With Map and
Illustrations. Crown 8vo, 4s.

Dick Cheveley : his Fortunes and Misfortunes. By W. H. G.
KINGSTON. 350 pp., square 16mo, and 22 full-page Illustrations.
Cloth, gilt edges, 7s. 6d.; plainer binding, plain edges, 5s.

Dick Sands, the Boy Captain. By JULES VERNE. With nearly
100 Illustrations, cloth, gilt, 10s. 6d.; plain binding and plain edges, 5s.

Don Quixote, Wit and Wisdom of. By EMMA THOMPSON.
Square fcap. 8vo, 3s. 6d.

Donnelly (F.) Atlantis in the Antediluvian World. Crown
8vo, 12s. 6d.

Dos Passos (F. R.) Law of Stockbrokers and Stock Exchanges.
8vo, 35s.

*E*GYPT. See "Senior," "De Leon," "Foreign Countries."

Eight Cousins. See ALCOTT.

Electric Lighting. A Comprehensive Treatise. By J. E. H.
GORDON. 8vo, fully Illustrated.   [*In preparation.*

Elementary History (An) of Art. Comprising Architecture,
Sculpture, Painting, and the Applied Arts. By N. D'ANVERS.
With a Preface by Professor ROGER SMITH. New Edition, illustrated
with upwards of 200 Wood Engravings. Crown 8vo, strongly bound
in cloth, price 10s. 6d.

Elementary History (An) of Music. Edited by OWEN J.
DULLEA. Illustrated with Portraits of the most eminent Composers,
and Engravings of the Musical Instruments of many Nations. Crown
8vo, cloth, 2s. 6d.

Elinor Dryden. By Mrs. MACQUOID. Crown 8vo, 6s.

Embroidery (Handbook of). Edited by LADY MARIAN ALFORD,
and published by authority of the Royal School of Art Needlework.
With 22 Coloured Plates, Designs, &c. Crown 8vo, 5s.

Emerson (R. W.) Life and Writings. Crown 8vo, 8s. 6d.

English Catalogue of Books. Vol. III., 1872—1880. Royal
8vo, half-morocco, 42s.

―――― *Dramatists of To-day.* By W. ARCHER, M.A. Crown
8vo, 8s. 6d.

English Philosophers. Edited by E. B. IVAN MÜLLER, M.A.

A series intended to give a concise view of the works and lives of English
thinkers. Crown 8vo volumes of 180 or 200 pp., price 3s. 6d. each.

Francis Bacon, by Thomas Fowler. | *John Stuart Mill, by Miss Helen
Hamilton, by W. H. S. Monck. | Taylor.
Hartley and James Mill, by G. S. | Shaftesbury and Hutcheson, by
Bower. | Professor Fowler.
| Adam Smith, by J. A. Farrer.

* *Not yet published.*

Episodes in the Life of an Indian Chaplain. Crown 8vo,
cloth extra, 12s. 6d.

Episodes of French History. Edited, with Notes, Maps, and Illustrations, by GUSTAVE MASSON, B.A. Small 8vo, 2*s.* 6*d.* each.
　I. **Charlemagne and the Carlovingians.**
　2. **Louis XI. and the Crusades.**
　3. **Part I. Francis I. and Charles V.**
　　,, **II. Francis I. and the Renaissance.**
　4. **Henry IV. and the End of the Wars of Religion.**

Erema ; or, My Father's Sin. 6*s.* *See* BLACKMORE.

Etcher (The). Containing 36 Examples of the Original Etched-work of Celebrated Artists, amongst others: BIRKET FOSTER, J. E. HODGSON, R.A., COLIN HUNTER, J. P. HESELTINE, ROBERT W. MACBETH, R. S. CHATTOCK, &c. Vols. for 1881 and 1882, imperial 4to, cloth extra, gilt edges, 2*l.* 12*s.* 6*d.* each.

Eton. ～ *See* "Day of my Life," "Out of School," "About Some Fellows."

*F*ARM *Ballads.* By WILL CARLETON. Boards, 1*s.* ; cloth, gilt edges, 1*s.* 6*d.*

Farm Festivals. By the same Author. Uniform with above.

Farm Legends. By the same Author. See above.

Fashion (History of). See "Challamel."

Fechner (G. T.) On Life after Death. 12mo, vellum, 2*s.* 6*d.*

Felkin (R. W.) and Wilson (Rev. C. T.) Uganda and the Egyptian Soudan. An Account of Travel in Eastern and Equatorial Africa ; including a Residence of Two Years at the Court of King Mtesa, and a Description of the Slave Districts of Bahr-el-Ghazel and Darfour. With a New Map of 1200 miles in these Provinces ; numerous Illustrations, and Notes. By R. W. FELKIN, F.R.G.S., &c., &c. ; and the Rev. C. T. WILSON, M.A. Oxon., F.R.G.S. 2 vols., crown 8vo, cloth, 28*s.*

Fern Paradise (The) : A Plea for the Culture of Ferns. By F. G. HEATH. New Edition, fully Illustrated, large post 8vo, cloth, gilt edges, 12*s.* 6*d.* Sixth Edition.

Fern World (The). By F. G. HEATH. Illustrated by Twelve Coloured Plates, giving complete Figures (Sixty-four in all) of every Species of British Fern, printed from Nature ; by several full-page and other Engravings. Cloth, gilt edges, 6th Edition, 12*s.* 6*d.*

Few Hints on Proving Wills (A). Enlarged Edition, 1*s.*

Fields (J. T.) Yesterdays with Authors. New Ed., 8vo., 16*s.*

First Steps in Conversational French Grammar. By F. JULIEN.
Being an Introduction to "Petites Leçons de Conversation et de
Grammaire," by the same Author. Fcap. 8vo, 128 pp., 1s.

Florence. See "Yriarte."

Flowers of Shakespeare. 32 beautifully Coloured Plates. 5s.

Four Lectures on Electric Induction. Delivered at the Royal
Institution, 1878-9. By J. E. H. GORDON, B.A. Cantab. With
numerous Illustrations. Cloth limp, square 16mo, 3s.

Foreign Countries and British Colonies. A series of Descriptive
Handbooks. Each volume will be the work of a writer who has
special acquaintance with the subject. Crown 8vo, 3s. 6d. each.

Australia, by J. F. Vesey Fitzgerald.
Austria, by D. Kay, F.R.G.S.
*Canada, by W. Fraser Rae.
Denmark and Iceland, by E. C.
Otté.
Egypt, by S. Lane Poole, B.A.
France, by Miss M. Roberts.
Greece, by L. Sergeant, B.A.
*Holland, by R. L. Poole.
Japan, by S. Mossman.
*New Zealand.
*Persia, by Major-Gen. Sir F. Gold-
smid.

Peru, by Clements R. Markham,
C.B.
Russia, by W. R. Morfill, M.A.
Spain, by Rev. Wentworth Webster.
Sweden and Norway, by F. H.
Woods.
*Switzerland, by W. A. P. Coolidg
M.A.
*Turkey-in-Asia, by J. C. McCoan,
M.P.
West Indies, by C. H. Eden,
F.R.G.S.

* Not ready yet.

Franc (Maud Jeanne). The following form one Series, small
post 8vo, in uniform cloth bindings, with gilt edges:—

Emily's Choice. 5s.
Hall's Vineyard. 4s.
John's Wife: A Story of Life in
South Australia. 4s.
Marian; or, The Light of Some
One's Home. 5s.
Silken Cords and Iron Fetters. 4s.

Vermont Vale. 5s.
Minnie's Mission. 4s.
Little Mercy. 5s.
Beatrice Melton's Discipline. 4s.
No Longer a Child. 4s.
Golden Gifts. 5s.
Two Sides to Every Question. 5s.

Francis (F.) War, Waves, and Wanderings, including a Cruise
in the "Lancashire Witch." 2 vols., crown 8vo, cloth extra, 24s.

Froissart (The Boy's). Selected from the Chronicles of England, France, Spain, &c. By SIDNEY LANIER. The Volume is
fully Illustrated, and uniform with "The Boy's King Arthur." Crown
8vo, cloth, 7s. 6d.

From Newfoundland to Manitoba; a Guide through Canada's
Maritime, Mining, and Prairie Provinces. By W. FRASER RAE.
Crown 8vo, with several Maps, 6s.

G*AMES of Patience.* See CADOGAN.

Gentle Life (Queen Edition). 2 vols. in 1, small 4to, 6s.

THE GENTLE LIFE SERIES.

Price 6s. each ; or in calf extra, price 10s. 6d. ; Smaller Edition, cloth extra, 2s. 6d.

The Gentle Life. Essays in aid of the Formation of Character of Gentlemen and Gentlewomen.

About in the World. Essays by Author of "The Gentle Life."

Like unto Christ. A New Translation of Thomas à Kempis' "De Imitatione Christi."

Familiar Words. An Index Verborum, or Quotation Handbook. 6s.

Essays by Montaigne. Edited and Annotated by the Author of "The Gentle Life."

The Gentle Life. 2nd Series.

The Silent Hour: Essays, Original and Selected. By the Author of "The Gentle Life."

Half-Length Portraits. Short Studies of Notable Persons. By J. HAIN FRISWELL.

Essays on English Writers, for the Self-improvement of Students in English Literature.

Other People's Windows. By J. HAIN FRISWELL.

A Man's Thoughts. By J. HAIN FRISWELL.

Gilder (W. H.) Schwatka's Search. Sledging in quest of the Franklin Records. Illustrated, 8vo, 12s. 6d.

Gilpin's Forest Scenery. Edited by F. G. HEATH. Large post 8vo, with numerous Illustrations. Uniform with "The Fern World," re-issued, 7s. 6d.

Gordon (J. E. H.). See "Four Lectures on Electric Induction," "Physical Treatise on Electricity," "Electric Lighting."

Gouffé. The Royal Cookery Book. By JULES GOUFFÉ ; translated and adapted for English use by ALPHONSE GOUFFÉ, Head Pastrycook to her Majesty the Queen. Illustrated with large plates printed in colours. 161 Woodcuts, 8vo, cloth extra, gilt edges, 2l. 2s.

—— Domestic Edition, half-bound, 10s. 6d.

"By far the ablest and most complete work on cookery that has ever been submitted to the gastronomical world."—*Pall Mall Gazette.*

Great Artists. See "Biographies."

Great Historic Galleries of England (The). Edited by LORD
RONALD GOWER, F.S.A., Trustee of the National Portrait Gallery.
Illustrated by 24 large and carefully executed *permanent* Photographs
of some of the most celebrated Pictures by the Great Masters. Vol. I.,
imperial 4to, cloth extra, gilt edges, 36*s.* Vol. II., with 36 large
permanent photographs, 2*l.* 12*s.* 6*d.*

Great Musicians. Edited by F. HUEFFER. A Series of
Biographies, crown 8vo, 3*s.* each :—

Bach.	*Handel.	Schubert.
*Beethoven.	*Mendelssohn.	*Schumann.
*Berlioz.	*Mozart.	Richard Wagner.
English Church Com-	Purcell.	Weber.
posers.	Rossini.	

* *In preparation.*

Green (N.) A Thousand Years Hence. Crown 8vo, 6*s.*

Grohmann (W. A. B.) Camps in the Rockies. 8vo, 12*s.* 6*d.*

Guizot's History of France. Translated by ROBERT BLACK.
Super-royal 8vo, very numerous Full-page and other Illustrations. In
8 vols., cloth extra, gilt, each 24*s.* This work is re-issued in cheaper
binding, 8 vols., at 10*s.* 6*d.* each.
"It supplies a want which has long been felt, and ought to be in the hands of all
students of history."—*Times.*

——————————— *Masson's School Edition.* The
History of France from the Earliest Times to the Outbreak of the
Revolution ; abridged from the Translation by Robert Black, M.A.,
with Chronological Index, Historical and Genealogical Tables, &c.
By Professor GUSTAVE MASSON, B.A., Assistant Master at Harrow
School. With 24 full-page Portraits, and many other Illustrations.
1 vol., demy 8vo, 600 pp., cloth extra, 10*s.* 6*d.*

Guizot's History of England. In 3 vols. of about 500 pp. each,
containing 60 to 70 Full-page and other Illustrations, cloth extra, gilt,
24*s.* each ; re-issue in cheaper binding, 10*s.* 6*d.* each.
"For luxury of typography, plainness of print, and beauty of illustration, these
volumes, of which but one has as yet appeared in English, will hold their own
against any production of an age so luxurious as our own in everything, typography
not excepted."—*Times.*

Guyon (Mde.) Life. By UPHAM. 6th Edition, crown 8vo, 6*s.*

HANDBOOK to the Charities of London. See LOW'S.

Hall (W. W.) How to Live Long ; or, 1408 *Health Maxims,*
Physical, Mental, and Moral. By W. W. HALL, A.M., M.D.
Small post 8vo, cloth, 2*s.* 2nd Edition.

Harper's Monthly Magazine. Published Monthly. 160 pages, fully Illustrated. 1*s.*
Vol. I. December, 1880, to May, 1881.
,, II. May, 1881, to November, 1881.
,, III. June to November, 1882.
Super-royal 8vo, 8*s.* 6*d.* each.

"'Harper's Magazine' is so thickly sown with excellent illustrations that to count them would be a work of time ; not that it is a picture magazine, for the engravings illustrate the text after the manner seen in some of our choicest *éditions de luxe.*"— *St. James's Gazette.*
"It is so pretty, so big, and so cheap. . . . An extraordinary shillingsworth— 160 large octavo pages, with over a score of articles, and more than three times as many illustrations."— *Edinburgh Daily Review.*
"An amazing shillingsworth . . . combining choice literature of both nations. '— *Nonconformist.*

*Hatton (Joseph) Journalistic London : Portraits and En-*gravings, with letterpress, of Distinguished Writers of the Day. Fcap. 4to, 12*s.* 6*d.*

———— *Three Recruits, and the Girls they left behind them.* Small post, 8vo, 6*s.*
"It hurries us along in unflagging excitement."—*Times.*

Heart of Africa. Three Years' Travels and Adventures in the Unexplored Regions of Central Africa, from 1868 to 1871. By Dr. GEORG SCHWEINFURTH. Numerous Illustrations, and large Map. 2 vols., crown 8vo, cloth, 15*s.*

Heath (Francis George). See "Autumnal Leaves," "Burnham Beeches," "Fern Paradise," "Fern World," "Gilpin's Forest Scenery," "Our Woodland Trees," "Peasant Life," "Sylvan Spring," "Trees and Ferns," "Where to Find Ferns."

Heber's (Bishop) Illustrated Edition of Hymns. With upwards of 100 beautiful Engravings. Small 4to, handsomely bound, 7*s.* 6*d.* Morocco, 18*s.* 6*d.* and 21*s.* New and Cheaper Edition, cloth, 3*s.* 6*d.*

Heir of Kilfinnan (The). By W. H. G. KINGSTON. With Illustrations. Cloth, gilt edges, 7*s.* 6*d.* ; plainer binding, plain edges, 5*s.*

Heldmann (Bernard) Mutiny on Board the Ship "Leander." Small post 8vo, gilt edges, numerous Illustrations, 7*s.* 6*d.*

Henty (G. A.) Winning his Spurs. Numerous Illustrations. Crown 8vo, 5*s.*

———— *Cornet of Horse ;* which see.

Herrick (Robert) Poetry. Preface by AUSTIN DOBSON. With numerous Illustrations, by E. A. ABBEY. 4to, gilt edges, 42*s.*

History of a Crime (The) ; Deposition of an Eye-witness. The Story of the Coup d'État. By VICTOR HUGO. Crown 8vo, 6*s.*

History of Ancient Art. Translated from the German of JOHN WINCKELMANN, by JOHN LODGE, M.D. With very numerous Plates and Illustrations. 2 vols., 8vo, 36s.

—— *England. See* GUIZOT.

—— *English Literature. See* SCHERR.

—— *Fashion.* Coloured Plates. 28s. *See* CHALLAMEL.

—— *France. See* GUIZOT.

—— *Russia. See* RAMBAUD.

—— *Merchant Shipping. See* LINDSAY.

—— *United States. See* BRYANT.

History and Principles of Weaving by Hand and by Power. With several hundred Illustrations. By ALFRED BARLOW. Royal 8vo, cloth extra, 1l. 5s. Second Edition.

Hitchman (Francis) Public Life of the Right Hon. Benjamin Disraeli, Earl of Beaconsfield. New Edition, with Portrait. Crown 8vo, 3s. 6d.

Holmes (O. W.) The Poetical Works of Oliver Wendell Holmes. In 2 vols., 18mo, exquisitely printed, and chastely bound in limp cloth, gilt tops, 10s. 6d.

Hoppus (J. D.) Riverside Papers. 2 vols., 12s.

Hovgaard (A.) See "Nordenskiöld's Voyage." 8vo, 21s.

How I Crossed Africa: from the Atlantic to the Indian Ocean, Through Unknown Countries; Discovery of the Great Zambesi Affluents, &c.—Vol. I., The King's Rifle. Vol. II., The Coillard Family. By Major SERPA PINTO. With 24 full-page and 118 half-page and smaller Illustrations, 13 small Maps, and 1 large one. 2 vols., demy 8vo, cloth extra, 42s.

How to get Strong and how to Stay so. By WILLIAM BLAIKIE. A Manual of Rational, Physical, Gymnastic, and other Exercises. With Illustrations, small post 8vo, 5s.

Hugo (Victor) "Ninety-Three." Illustrated. Crown 8vo, 6s.

—— *Toilers of the Sea.* Crown 8vo. Illustrated, 6s.; fancy boards, 2s.; cloth, 2s. 6d.; on large paper with all the original Illustrations, 10s. 6d.

—— *and his Times.* Translated from the French of A. BARBOU by ELLEN E. FREWER. 120 Illustrations, many of them from designs by Victor Hugo himself. Super-royal 8vo, cloth extra, 24s.

—— *See* "History of a Crime."

Hundred Greatest Men (The). 8 portfolios, 21*s*. each, or 4
vols., half-morocco, gilt edges, 12 guineas, containing 15 to 20
Portraits each. See below.

> "Messrs. SAMPSON LOW & Co. are about to issue an important 'International'
> work, entitled, 'THE HUNDRED GREATEST MEN;' being the Lives and
> Portraits of the 100 Greatest Men of History, divided into Eight Classes, each Class
> to form a Monthly Quarto Volume. The Introductions to the volumes are to be
> written by recognized authorities on the different subjects, the English contributors
> being DEAN STANLEY, Mr. MATTHEW ARNOLD, Mr. FROUDE, and Professor MAX
> MÜLLER: in Germany, Professor HELMHOLTZ; in France, MM. TAINE and
> RENAN; and in America, Mr. EMERSON. The Portraits are to be Reproductions
> from fine and rare Steel Engravings."—*Academy.*

Hygiene and Public Health (A Treatise on). Edited by A. H.
BUCK, M.D. Illustrated by numerous Wood Engravings. In 2
royal 8vo vols., cloth, One guinea each.

Hymnal Companion to Book of Common Prayer. See
BICKERSTETH.

ILLUSTRATED Text-Books of Art-Education. Edited by
EDWARD J. POYNTER, R.A. Each Volume contains numerous Illus-
trations, and is strongly bound for the use of Students, price 5*s*. The
Volumes now ready are:—

PAINTING.

Classic and Italian. By PERCY
R. HEAD.
German, Flemish, and Dutch.

French and Spanish.
English and American.

ARCHITECTURE.

Classic and Early Christian.
Gothic and Renaissance. By T. ROGER SMITH.

SCULPTURE.

Antique: Egyptian and Greek. | Renaissance and Modern.
Italian Sculptors of the 14th and 15th Centuries.

ORNAMENT.

Decoration in Colour. | Architectural Ornament.

Illustrated Dictionary (An) of Words used in Art and
Archæology. Explaining Terms frequently used in Works of
Architecture, Arms, Bronzes, Christian Art, Colour, Costume, Deco
ration, Devices, Emblems, Heraldry, Lace, Personal Ornaments
Pottery, Painting, Sculpture, &c., with their Derivations. By J. W.
MOLLETT, B.A., Officier de l'Instruction Publique (France); Author
of "Life of Rembrandt," &c. Illustrated with 600 Wood Engravings.
Small 4to, strongly bound in cloth, 15*s*.

In my Indian Garden. By PHIL ROBINSON, Author of "Under
the Punkah." With a Preface by EDWIN ARNOLD, M.A., C.S.I., &c.
Crown 8vo, limp cloth, 4th Edition, 3*s*. 6*d*.

Irving (*Washington*). Complete Library Edition of his Works in 27 Vols., Copyright, Unabridged, and with the Author's Latest Revisions, called the "Geoffrey Crayon" Edition, handsomely printed in large square 8vo, on superfine laid paper, and each volume, of about 500 pages, will be fully Illustrated. 12*s.* 6*d.* per vol. *See also* "Little Britain."

—————————— ("American Men of Letters.") 2*s.* 6*d.*

JAMES (*C.*) *Curiosities of Law and Lawyers.* 8vo, 7*s.* 6*d.*

Johnson (*O.*) *William Lloyd Garrison and his Times.* Crown 8vo, 12*s.* 6*d.*

Jones (*Major*) *The Emigrants' Friend.* A Complete Guide to the United States. New Edition. 2*s.* 6*d.*

KEMPIS (*Thomas à*) *Daily Text-Book.* Square 16mo, 2*s.* 6*d.*; interleaved as a Birthday Book, 3*s.* 6*d.*

Kingston (*W. H. G.*). *See* "Snow-Shoes," "Child of the Cavern," "Two Supercargoes," "With Axe and Rifle," "Begum's Fortune." "Heir of Kilfinnan," "Dick Cheveley." Each vol., with very numerous Illustrations, square crown 16mo, gilt edges, 7*s.* 6*d.*; plainer binding, plain edges, 5*s.*

LADY Silverdale's Sweetheart. 6*s.* *See* BLACK.

Lanier. See "Boy's Froissart," "King Arthur," &c.

Lansdell (*H.*) *Through Siberia.* 2 vols., demy 8vo, 30*s.*; New Edition, very numerous illustrations, 8vo, 15*s.*

Larden (*W.*) *School Course on Heat.* Illustrated, crown 8vo, 5*s.*

Lathrop (*G. P.*) *In the Distance.* 2 vols., crown 8vo, 21*s.*

Lectures on Architecture. By E. VIOLLET-LE-DUC. Translated by BENJAMIN BUCKNALL, Architect. With 33 Steel Plates and 200 Wood Engravings. Super-royal 8vo, leather back, gilt top, with complete Index, 2 vols., 3*l.* 3*s.*

Leyland (*R. W.*) *A Holiday in South Africa.* Crown 8vo 12*s.* 6*d.*

Library of Religious Poetry. A Collection of the Best Poems of all Ages and Tongues. Edited by PHILIP SCHAFF, D.D., LL.D., and ARTHUR GILMAN, M.A. Royal 8vo, 1036 pp., cloth extra, gilt edges, 21*s.*; re-issue in cheaper binding, 10*s. 6d.*

Lindsay (W. S.) History of Merchant Shipping and Ancient Commerce. Over 150 Illustrations, Maps, and Charts. In 4 vols., demy 8vo, cloth extra. Vols. 1 and 2, 11*s.*; vols. 3 and 4, 14*s.* each. 4 vols. complete for 50*s.*

Little Britain; together with *The Spectre Bridegroom,* and *A* Legend of Sleepy Hollow. By WASHINGTON IRVING. An entirely New *Edition de luxe,* specially suitable for Presentation. Illustrated by 120 very fine Engravings on Wood, by Mr. J. D. COOPER. Designed by Mr. CHARLES O. MURRAY. Re-issue, square crown 8vo, cloth, 6*s.*

Long (Mrs. W. H. C.) Peace and War in the Transvaal. 12mo, 3*s. 6d.*

Lorna Doone. 6*s.,* 31*s. 6d.,* 35*s.* See "Blackmore."

Low's Select Novelets. Small post 8vo, cloth extra, 3*s. 6d.* each.

> **Friends : a Duet.** By E. S. PHELPS, Author of "The Gates Ajar."
> **Baby Rue : Her Adventures and Misadventures, her Friends** and her Enemies. By CHARLES M. CLAY.
> **The Story of Helen Troy.**
> "A pleasant book."—*Truth.*
> **The Clients of Dr. Bernagius.** From the French of LUCIEN BIART, by Mrs. CASHEL HOEY.
> **The Undiscovered Country.** By W. D. HOWELLS.
> **A Gentleman of Leisure.** By EDGAR FAWCETT.

Low's Standard Library of Travel and Adventure. Crown 8vo, bound uniformly in cloth extra, price 7*s. 6d.,* except where price is given.

1. **The Great Lone Land.** By Major W. F. BUTLER, C.B.
2. **The Wild North Land.** By Major W. F. BUTLER, C.B.
3. **How I found Livingstone.** By H. M. STANLEY.
4. **Through the Dark Continent.** By H. M. STANLEY. 12*s. 6d.*
5. **The Threshold of the Unknown Region.** By C. R. MARK-HAM. (4th Edition, with Additional Chapters, 10*s. 6d.*)
6. **Cruise of the Challenger.** By W. J. J. SPRY, R.N.
7. **Burnaby's On Horseback through Asia Minor.** 10*s. 6d.*
8. **Schweinfurth's Heart of Africa.** 2 vols., 15*s.*
9. **Marshall's Through America.**

Low's Standard Novels. Crown 8vo, 6s. each, cloth extra.

Work. A Story of Experience. By LOUISA M. ALCOTT.
A Daughter of Heth. By W. BLACK.
In Silk Attire. By W. BLACK.
Kilmeny. A Novel. By W. BLACK.
Lady Silverdale's Sweetheart. By W. BLACK.
Sunrise. By W. BLACK.
Three Feathers. By WILLIAM BLACK.
Alice Lorraine. By R. D. BLACKMORE.
Christowell, a Dartmoor Tale. By R. D. BLACKMORE.
Clara Vaughan. By R. D. BLACKMORE.
Cradock Nowell. By R. D. BLACKMORE.
Cripps the Carrier. By R. D. BLACKMORE.
Erema; or, My Father's Sin. By R. D. BLACKMORE.
Lorna Doone. By R. D. BLACKMORE.
Mary Anerley. By R. D. BLACKMORE.
An English Squire. By Miss COLERIDGE.
Mistress Judith. A Cambridgeshire Story. By C. C. FRASER-TYTLER.
A Story of the Dragonnades; or, Asylum Christi. By the Rev. E. GILLIAT, M.A.
A Laodicean. By THOMAS HARDY.
Far from the Madding Crowd. By THOMAS HARDY.
The Hand of Ethelberta. By THOMAS HARDY.
The Trumpet Major. By THOMAS HARDY.
Three Recruits. By JOSEPH HATTON.
A Golden Sorrow. By Mrs. CASHEL HOEY. New Edition.
Out of Court. By Mrs. CASHEL HOEY.
History of a Crime: The Story of the Coup d'État. VICTOR HUGO.
Ninety-Three. By VICTOR HUGO. Illustrated.
Adela Cathcart. By GEORGE MAC DONALD.
Guild Court. By GEORGE MAC DONALD.
Mary Marston. By GEORGE MAC DONALD.
Stephen Archer. New Edition of "Gifts." By GEORGE MAC DONALD.
The Vicar's Daughter. By GEORGE MAC DONALD.
Weighed and Wanting. By GEORGE MAC DONALD.
[In the Press.
Diane. By Mrs. MACQUOID.
Elinor Dryden. By Mrs. MACQUOID.
My Lady Greensleeves. By HELEN MATHERS.
John Holdsworth. By W. CLARK RUSSELL.
A Sailor's Sweetheart. By W. CLARK RUSSELL.
Wreck of the Grosvenor. By W. CLARK RUSSELL.
The Afghan Knife. By R. A. STERNDALE.
My Wife and I. By Mrs. BEECHER STOWE.
Poganuc People, Their Loves and Lives. By Mrs. B. STOWE.
Ben Hur: a Tale of the Christ. By LEW. WALLACE.

Low's Handbook to the Charities of London (Annual). Edited and revised to date by C. MACKESON, F.S.S., Editor of "A Guide to the Churches of London and its Suburbs," &c. Paper, 1*s.*; cloth, 1*s.* 6*d.*

MAC DONALD (G.) Orts. Small post 8vo, 6*s.*

—— See also "Low's Standard Novels."

Macgregor (John) "Rob Roy" on the Baltic. 3rd Edition, small post 8vo, 2*s.* 6*d.*; cloth, gilt edges, 3*s.* 6*d.*

—— *A Thousand Miles in the "Rob Roy" Canoe.* 11th Edition, small post 8vo, 2*s.* 6*d.*; cloth, gilt edges, 3*s.* 6*d.*

—— *Description of the "Rob Roy" Canoe,* with Plans, &c., 1*s.*

—— *The Voyage Alone in the Yawl "Rob Roy."* New Edition, thoroughly revised, with additions, small post 8vo, 5*s.*; boards, 2*s.* 6*d.*

Macquoid (Mrs.). *See* Low's STANDARD NOVELS.

Magazine. *See* HARPER, UNION JACK, THE ETCHER, MEN OF MARK.

Magyarland. *A Narrative of Travels through the Snowy Carpathians,* and Great Alföld of the Magyar. By a Fellow of the Carpathian Society (Diploma of 1881), and Author of "The Indian Alps." 2 vols., 8vo, cloth extra, with about 120 Woodcuts from the Author's own sketches and drawings, 38*s.*

Manitoba : its History, Growth, and Present Position. By the Rev. Professor BRYCE, Principal of Manitoba College, Winnipeg. Crown 8vo, with Illustrations and Maps, 7*s.* 6*d.*

Markham (C. R.) The Threshold of the Unknown Region. Crown 8vo, with Four Maps, 4th Edition. Cloth extra, 10*s.* 6*d.*

Markham (C. R.) War between Peru and Chili, 1879-1881. Crown 8vo, with four Maps, &c. *[In preparation.*

Marshall (W. G.) Through America. New Edition, crown 8vo, with about 100 Illustrations, 7*s.* 6*d.*

Martin (J. W.) Float Fishing and Spinning in the Nottingham Style. Crown 8vo, 2*s.* 6*d.*

Marvin (Charles) The Russian Advance towards India. 8vo, 16*s.*

Maury (Commander) Physical Geography of the Sea, and its
Meteorology. Being a Reconstruction and Enlargement of his former
Work, with Charts and Diagrams. New Edition, crown 8vo, 6s.

Memoirs of Madame de Rémusat, 1802—1808. By her Grandson, M. PAUL DE RÉMUSAT, Senator. Translated by Mrs. CASHEL
HOEY and Mr. JOHN LILLIE. 4th Edition, cloth extra. This
work was written by Madame de Rémusat during the time she
was living on the most intimate terms with the Empress Josephine,
and is full of revelations respecting the private life of Bonaparte, and
of men and politics of the first years of the century. Revelations
which have already created a great sensation in Paris. 8vo, 2 vols., 32s.

—— *See also* " Selection."

Ménus (366, one for each day of the year). Each Ménu is given
in French and English, with the recipe for making every dish
mentioned. Translated from the French of COUNT BRISSE, by Mrs.
MATTHEW CLARKE. Crown 8vo, 5s.

Men of Mark: a Gallery of Contemporary Portraits of the most
Eminent Men of the Day taken from Life, especially for this publication, price 1s. 6d. monthly. Vols. I. to VII., handsomely bound,
cloth, gilt edges, 25s. each.

Mendelssohn Family (The), 1729—1847. From Letters and
Journals. Translated from the German of SEBASTIAN HENSEL.
3rd Edition, 2 vols., demy 8vo, 30s.

Michael Strogoff. See VERNE.

Mitford (Miss). See " Our Village."

Modern Etchings of Celebrated Paintings. 4to, 31s. 6d.

Mollett (J. W.) Illustrated Dictionary of Words used in Art
and Archæology. Small 4to, 15s.

Morley (H.) English Literature in the Reign of Victoria. The
2000th volume of the Tauchnitz Collection of Authors. 18mo, 2s. 6d.

Music. See " Great Musicians."

NARRATIVES of State Trials in the Nineteenth Century.
First Period: From the Union with Ireland to the Death of
George IV., 1801—1830. By G. LATHOM BROWNE, of the Middle Temple,
Barrister-at-Law. 2nd Edition, 2 vols., crown 8vo, cloth, 26s.

Nature and Functions of Art (The); and more especially of
Architecture. By LEOPOLD EIDLITZ. Medium 8vo, cloth, 21s.

Naval Brigade in South Africa (The). By HENRY F. NOR-
BURY, C.B., R.N. Crown 8vo, cloth extra, 10s. 6d.

New Child's Play (*A*). Sixteen Drawings by E. V. B. Beautifully printed in colours, 4to, cloth extra, 12s. 6d.

Newfoundland. By FRASER RAE. See " From Newfoundland."

New Novels. Crown 8vo, cloth, 10s. 6d. per vol. :—
  The Granvilles. By the Hon. E. TALBOT. 3 vols.
  One of Us. By E. RANDOLPH.
  Weighed and Wanting. By GEORGE MAC DONALD. 3 vols.
  Castle Warlock. By GEORGE MAC DONALD. 3 vols.
  Under the Downs. By E. GILLIAT. 3 vols.
  A Stranger in a Strange Land. By LADY CLAY. 3 vols.
  The Heart of Erin. By Miss OWENS BLACKBURN. 3 vols.
  A Chelsea Householder. 3 vols.
  Two on a Tower. By THOMAS HARDY. 3 vols.
  The Lady Maud. By W. CLARK RUSSELL. 3 vols.

Nice and Her Neighbours. By the Rev. CANON HOLE, Author
of " A Book about Roses," " A Little Tour in Ireland," &c. Small
4to, with numerous choice Illustrations, 12s. 6d.

Noah's Ark. A Contribution to the Study of Unnatural History.
By PHIL ROBINSON. Small post 8vo, 12s. 6d.

Noble Words and Noble Deeds. From the French of E. MULLER.
Containing many Full-page Illustrations by PHILIPPOTEAUX. Square
imperial 16mo, cloth extra, 7s. 6d. ; plainer binding, plain edges, 5s.

Nordenskiöld's Voyage around Asia and Europe. A Popular
Account of the North-East Passage of the " Vega." By Lieut. A.
HOVGAARD, of the Royal Danish Navy, and member of the " Vega "
Expedition. 8vo, with about 50 Illustrations and 3 Maps, 21s.

Nordhoff (*C.*) *California, for Health, Pleasure, and Residence.*
New Edition, 8vo, with Maps and Illustrations, 12s. 6d.

Nothing to Wear ; and Two Millions. By W. A. BUTLER.
New Edition. Small post 8vo, in stiff coloured wrapper, 1s.

Nursery Playmates (*Prince of*). 217 Coloured Pictures for
Children by eminent Artists. Folio, in coloured boards, 6s.

OFF to the Wilds : A Story for Boys. By G. MANVILLE
FENN. Profusely Illustrated. Crown 8vo, 7s. 6d.

Old-Fashioned Girl. See ALCOTT.

On Horseback through Asia Minor. By Capt. FRED BURNABY.
2 vols., 8vo, 38s. Cheaper Edition, crown 8vo, 10s. 6d.

Our Little Ones in Heaven. Edited by the Rev. H. ROBBINS.
With Frontispiece after Sir JOSHUA REYNOLDS. Fcap., cloth extra,
New Edition—the 3rd, with Illustrations, 5s.

Our Village. By MARY RUSSELL MITFORD. Illustrated with Frontispiece Steel Engraving, and 12 full-page and 157 smaller Cuts. Crown 4to, cloth, gilt edges, 21s.; cheaper binding, 10s. 6d.

Our Woodland Trees. By F. G. HEATH. Large post 8vo, cloth, gilt edges, uniform with "Fern World" and "Fern Paradise," by the same Author. 8 Coloured Plates (showing leaves of every British Tree) and 20 Woodcuts, cloth, gilt edges, 12s. 6d. New Edition. About 600 pages.

Outlines of Ornament in all Styles. A Work of Reference for the Architect, Art Manufacturer, Decorative Artist, and Practical Painter. By W. and G. A. AUDSLEY, Fellows of the Royal Institute of British Architects. Only a limited number have been printed and the stones destroyed. Small folio, 60 plates, with introductory text, cloth gilt, 31s. 6d.

PALLISER (Mrs.) A History of Lace, from the Earliest Period. A New and Revised Edition, with additional cuts and text, upwards of 100 Illustrations and coloured Designs. 1 vol., 8vo, 1l. 1s.

—— *Historic Devices, Badges, and War Cries.* 8vo, 1l. 1s.

—— *The China Collector's Pocket Companion.* With upwards of 1000 Illustrations of Marks and Monograms. 2nd Edition, with Additions. Small post 8vo, limp cloth, 5s.

Pathways of Palestine: a Descriptive Tour through the Holy Land. By the Rev. CANON TRISTRAM. Illustrated with 44 permanent Photographs. (The Photographs are large, and most perfect Specimens of the Art.) Vols. I. and II., folio, gilt edges, 31s. 6d. each.

Peasant Life in the West of England. By FRANCIS GEORGE HEATH, Author of "Sylvan Spring," "The Fern World." Crown 8vo, 400 pp. (with Facsimile of Autograph Letter from Lord Beaconsfield to the Author, written December 28, 1880), 10s. 6d.

Petites Leçons de Conversation et de Grammaire · *Oral and* Conversational Method; the most Useful Topics ot Conversation. By F. JULIEN. Cloth, 3s. 6d.

Photography (History and Handbook of). See TISSANDIER.

Physical Treatise on Electricity and Magnetism. By J. E. H. GORDON, B.A. With about 200 coloured, full-page, and other Illustrations. 2 vols., 8vo. New Edition. [*In preparation.*

Poems of the Inner Life. Chiefly from Modern Authors. Small 8vo, 5s.

Poganuc People: their Loves and Lives. By Mrs. BEECHER STOWE. Crown 8vo, cloth, 6s.

Polar Expeditions. *See* KOLDEWEY, MARKHAM, MACGAHAN, NARES, and NORDENSKIÖLD.

Poynter (Edward J., R.A.). *See* "Illustrated Text-books."

Prudence: a Story of Æsthetic London. By LUCY E. LILLIE. Small 8vo, 5s.

Publishers' Circular (The), and General Record of British and Foreign Literature. Published on the 1st and 15th of every Month, 3d.

Pyrenees (The). By HENRY BLACKBURN. With 100 Illustrations by GUSTAVE DORÉ, corrected to 1881. Crown 8vo, 7s. 6d.

R*AE (F.) Newfoundland.* See "From."

Redford (G.) Ancient Sculpture. Crown 8vo, 5s.

Reid (T. W.) Land of the Bey. Post 8vo, 10s. 6d.

Rémusat (Madame de). *See* "Memoirs of," "Selection."

Richter (Jean Paul). *The Literary Works of Leonardo da* Vinci. Containing his Writings on Painting, Sculpture, and Architecture, his Philosophical Maxims, Humorous Writings, and Miscellaneous Notes on Personal Events, on his Contemporaries, on Literature, &c. ; for the first time published from Autograph Manuscripts. By J. P. RICHTER, Ph.Dr., Hon. Member of the Royal and Imperial Academy of Rome, &c. 2 vols., imperial 8vo, containing about 200 Drawings in Autotype Reproductions, and numerous other Illustrations. Price Eight Guineas to Subscribers. After publication the price will be Twelve Guineas.

———— *Italian Art in the National Gallery.* 4to. Illustrated. Cloth gilt, 2l. 2s.; half-morocco, uncut, 2l. 12s. 6d.

Robinson (Phil). *See* "In my Indian Garden," "Under the Punkah," "Noah's Ark," "Sinners and Saints." .

Rose (F.) Complete Practical Machinist. New Edition, 12mo, 12s. 6d.

Rose Library (The). Popular Literature of all Countries. Each volume, 1s.; cloth, 2s. 6d. Many of the Volumes are Illustrated—
Little Women. By LOUISA M. ALCOTT.
Little Women Wedded. Forming a Sequel to "Little Women."
Little Men. By L. M. ALCOTT. Dble. vol., 2s.; cloth gilt, 3s. 6d.
An Old-Fashioned Girl. By LOUISA M. ALCOTT. Double vol., 2s.; cloth, 3s. 6d.
Work. A Story of Experience. By L. M. ALCOTT.
Beginning Again. Sequel to "Work." By L. M. ALCOTT.
Stowe (Mrs. H. B.) The Pearl of Orr's Island.
———— The Minister's Wooing.

Rose Library (continued) :—

Stowe (Mrs. H. B.) We and our Neighbours. Double vol., 2s
cloth, 3s. 6d.

—— My Wife and I. Double vol., 2s. ; cloth gilt, 3s. 6d.

Hans Brinker ; or, the Silver Skates. By Mrs. DODGE.

My Study Windows. By J. R. LOWELL.

The Guardian Angel. By OLIVER WENDELL HOLMES.

My Summer in a Garden. By C. D. WARNER.

Dred Mrs BEECHER STOWE. Dble. vol., 2s.; cloth gilt, 3s. 6d.

Farm Ballads. By WILL CARLETON.

Farm Festivals. By WILL CARLETON.

Farm Legends. By WILL CARLETON.

The Clients of Dr. Bernagius. 2 parts, 1s. each.

The Undiscovered Country. By W. D. HOWELLS.

Baby Rue By C. M. CLAY.

The Rose in Bloom. By L. M. ALCOTT. 2s. ; cloth gilt, 3s. 6d.

Eight Cousins. By L. M. ALCOTT. 2s. ; cloth gilt, 3s. 6d.

Under the Lilacs. By L. M. ALCOTT. 2s. ; cloth gilt, 3s. 6d.

Silver Pitchers. By LOUISA M. ALCOTT.

Jemmy's Cruise in the "Pinafore," and other Tales. By
LOUISA M. ALCOTT. 2s.; cloth gilt, 3s. 6d.

Jack and Jill. By LOUISA M. ALCOTT. 2s.; cloth gilt, 3s. 6d.

Hitherto. By the Author of the "Gayworthys." 2 vols., 1s. each.

Friends : a Duet. By E. STUART PHELPS.

A Gentleman of Leisure. A Novel. By EDGAR FAWCETT.

The Story of Helen Troy.

Round the Yule Log : Norwegian Folk and Fairy Tales.
Translated from the Norwegian of P. CHR. ASBJÖRNSEN. With 100
Illustrations after drawings by Norwegian Artists, and an Introduction
by E. W. Gosse. Imperial 16mo, cloth extra, gilt edges, 7s 6d.

Rousselet (Louis) Son of the Constable of France. Small post
8vo, numerous Illustrations, 5s.

—— *The Drummer Boy : a Story of the Days of Washington.*
Small post 8vo, numerous Illustrations, 5s.

Russell (W. Clark) The Lady Maud. 3 vols., crown 8vo,
31s. 6d.

—— *See also* LOW'S STANDARD NOVELS *and* WRECK.

Russell (W. H., LL.D.) Hesperothen : Notes from the Western
World. A Record of a Ramble through part of the United States,
Canada, and the Far West, in the Spring and Summer of 1881. By
W. H. RUSSELL, LL.D. 2 vols., crown 8vo, cloth, 24s.

—— *The Tour of the Prince of Wales in India.* By
W. H. RUSSELL, LL.D. Fully Illustrated by SYDNEY P. HALL,
M.A. Super-royal 8vo, cloth extra, gilt edges, 52s. 6d.; Large
Paper Edition, 84s.

Russian Literature. See "Turner."

S*AINTS and their Symbols: A Companion in the Churches* and Picture Galleries of Europe. With Illustrations. Royal 16mo, cloth extra, 3*s.* 6*d.*

Scherr (Prof. J.) History of English Literature. Translated from the German. Crown 8vo, 8*s.* 6*d.*

Schuyler (Eugène). The Life of Peter the Great. By EUGÈNE SCHUYLER, Author of "Turkestan." 2 vols., demy 8vo.
[*In preparation.*]

Scott (Leader) Renaissance of Art in Italy. 4to, 31*s.* 6*d.*

Selection from the Letters of Madame de Rémusat to her Husband and Son, from 1804 to 1813. From the French, by Mrs. CASHEL HOEY and Mr. JOHN LILLIE. In 1 vol., demy 8vo (uniform with the "Memoirs of Madame de Rémusat," 2 vols.), cloth extra, 16*s.*

Senior (Nassau W.) Conversations and Journals in Egypt and Malta. 2 vols., 8vo, 24*s.*
These volumes contain conversations with SAID PASHA, ACHIM BEY, HEKEKYAN BEY, the Patriarch, M. DE LESSEPS, M. ST. HILAIRE, Sir FREDERICK BRUCE, Sir ADRIAN DINGLI, and many other remarkable people.

Seonee: Sporting in the Satpura Range of Central India, and in the Valley of the Nerbudda. By R. A. STERNDALE, F.R.G.S. 8vo, with numerous Illustrations, 21*s.*

Shadbolt (S.) The Afghan Campaigns of 1878—1880. By SYDNEY SHADBOLT, Joint Author of "The South African Campaign of 1879." 2 vols., royal quarto, cloth extra, 3*l.* 3*s.*

Shooting: its Appliances, Practice, and Purpose. By JAMES DALZIEL DOUGALL, F.S.A., F.Z.A., Author of "Scottish Field Sports," &c. New Edition, revised with additions. Crown 8vo, cloth extra, 7*s.* 6*d.*
"The book is admirable in every way. . . . . We wish it every success."—*Globe.*
"A very complete treatise. . . . . Likely to take high rank as an authority on shooting."—*Daily News.*

Sikes (Wirt). Rambles and Studies in Old South Wales. With numerous Illustrations. Demy 8vo, 18*s.*

Silent Hour (The). See "Gentle Life Series."

Silver Sockets (The); and other Shadows of Redemption. Eighteen Sermons preached in Christ Church, Hampstead, by the Rev. C. H. WALLER. Small post 8vo, cloth, 6*s.*

Sinners and Saints: a Tour across the United States of America, and Round them. By PHIL ROBINSON. [*In the Press.*]

Sir Roger de Coverley. Re-imprinted from the "Spectator." With 125 Woodcuts, and steel Frontispiece specially designed and engraved for the Work. Small fcap. 4to, 6*s.*

Smith (G.) Assyrian Explorations and Discoveries. By the late GEORGE SMITH. Illustrated by Photographs and Woodcuts. Demy 8vo, 6th Edition, 18s.

—— *The Chaldean Account of Genesis.* By the late G. SMITH, of the Department of Oriental Antiquities, British Museum. With many Illustrations. Demy 8vo, cloth extra, 6th Edition, 16s. An entirely New Edition, completely revised and re-written by the Rev. PROFESSOR SAYCE, Queen's College, Oxford. Demy 8vo, 18s.

Smith (J. Moyr). See "Ancient Greek Female Costume."

Snow-Shoes and Canoes; or, the Adventures of a Fur-Hunter in the Hudson's Bay Territory. By W. H. G. KINGSTON. 2nd Edition. With numerous Illustrations. Square crown 8vo, cloth extra, gilt edges, 7s. 6d. ; plainer binding, 5s.

South African Campaign, 1879 (The). Compiled by J. P. MACKINNON (formerly 72nd Highlanders), and S. H. SHADBOLT ; and dedicated, by permission, to Field-Marshal H.R.H. The Duke of Cambridge. Containing a portrait and biography of every officer killed in the campaign. 4to, handsomely bound in cloth extra, 2l. 10s.

South Kensington Museum. Vol. II., 21s.

Stack (E.) Six Months in Persia. 2 vols., crown 8vo, 24s.

Stanley (H. M.) How I Found Livingstone. Crown 8vo, cloth extra, 7s. 6d. ; large Paper Edition, 10s. 6d.

—— *"My Kalulu," Prince, King, and Slave.* A Story from Central Africa. Crown 8vo, about 430 pp., with numerous graphic Illustrations, after Original Designs by the Author. Cloth, 7s. 6d.

—— *Coomassie and Magdala.* A Story of Two British Campaigns in Africa. Demy 8vo, with Maps and Illustrations, 16s.

—— *Through the Dark Continent.* Cheaper Edition, crown 8vo, 12s. 6d.

State Trials. See "Narratives."

Stenhouse (Mrs.) An Englishwoman in Utah. Crown 8vo, 2s. 6d.

Stoker (Bram) Under the Sunset. Crown 8vo, 6s.

Story without an End. From the German of Carové, by the late Mrs. SARAH T. AUSTIN. Crown 4to, with 15 Exquisite Drawings by E. V. B., printed in Colours in Fac-simile of the original Water Colours ; and numerous other Illustrations. New Edition, 7s. 6d.

—— square 4to, with Illustrations by HARVEY. 2s. 6d.

Stowe (Mrs. Beecher) Dred. Cheap Edition, boards, 2s. Cloth, gilt edges, 3s. 6d.

Stowe (*Mrs Beecher*) *Footsteps of the Master.* With Illustrations and red borders. Small post 8vo, cloth extra, 6s.

———— *Geography*, with 60 Illustrations. Square cloth, 4s. 6d.

———— *Little Foxes.* Cheap Edition, 1s.; Library Edition, 4s. 6d.

———— *Betty's Bright Idea.* 1s.

———— *My Wife and I; or, Harry Henderson's History.* Small post 8vo, cloth extra, 6s.*

———— *Minister's Wooing.* 5s.; Copyright Series, 1s. 6d.; cl., 2s.*

———— *Old Town Folk.* 6s.; Cheap Edition, 2s. 6d.

———— *Old Town Fireside Stories.* Cloth extra, 3s. 6d.

———— *Our Folks at Poganuc.* 6s.

———— *We and our Neighbours.* 1 vol., small post 8vo, 6s. Sequel to "My Wife and I."*

———— *Pink and White Tyranny.* Small post 8vo, 3s. 6d. Cheap Edition, 1s. 6d. and 2s.

———— *Queer Little People.* 1s.; cloth, 2s.

———— *Chimney Corner.* 1s.; cloth, 1s. 6d.

———— *The Pearl of Orr's Island.* Crown 8vo, 5s.*

———— *Woman in Sacred History.* Illustrated with 15 Chromo-lithographs and about 200 pages of Letterpress. Demy 4to, cloth extra, gilt edges, 25s.

Student's French Examiner. By F. JULIEN, Author of "Petites Leçons de Conversation et de Grammaire." Square cr. 8vo, cloth, 2s.

Studies in the Theory of Descent. By Dr. AUG. WEISMANN, Professor in the University of Freiburg. Translated and edited by RAPHAEL MELDOLA, F.C.S., Secretary of the Entomological Society of London. Part I.—"On the Seasonal Dimorphism of Butterflies," containing Original Communications by Mr. W. H. EDWARDS, of Coalburgh. With two Coloured Plates. Price of Part I. (to Subscribers for the whole work only), 8s.; Part II. (6 coloured plates), 16s.; Part III., 6s. Complete, 2 vols., 40s.

Surgeon's Handbook on the Treatment of Wounded in War. By Dr. FRIEDRICH ESMARCH, Surgeon-General to the Prussian Army. Numerous Coloured Plates and Illustrations, 8vo, strongly bound, 1l. 8s.

* *See also* Rose Library.

Sylvan Spring. By FRANCIS GEORGE HEATH. Illustrated by 12 Coloured Plates, drawn by F. E. HULME, F.L.S., Artist and Author of " Familiar Wild Flowers;" by 16 full-page, and more than 100 other Wood Engravings. Large post 8vo, cloth, gilt edges, 12s. 6d.

TAHITI. By Lady BRASSEY, Author of the " Voyage of the Sunbeam." With 31 Autotype Illustrations after Photos. by Colonel STUART-WORTLEY. Fcap. 4to, very tastefully bound, 21s.

Taine (H. A.) "Les Origines de la France Contemporaine." Translated by JOHN DURAND.

Vol. 1. **The Ancient Regime.** Demy 8vo, cloth, 16s.
Vol. 2. **The French Revolution.** Vol. 1. do.
Vol. 3. **Do. do.** Vol. 2. do.

Tauchnitz's English Editions of German Authors. Each volume, cloth flexible, 2s. ; or sewed, 1s. 6d. (Catalogues post free on application.)

—— (B.) *German and English Dictionary.* Cloth, 1s. 6d.; roan, 2s.

—— *French and English Dictionary.* Paper, 1s. 6d.; cloth, 2s.; roan, 2s. 6d.

—— *Italian and English Dictionary.* Paper, 1s. 6d.; cloth, 2s. ; roan, 2s. 6d.

—— *Spanish and English.* Paper, 1s. 6d. ; cloth, 2s. ; roan, 2s. 6d.

Taylor (W. M.) Paul the Missionary. Crown 8vo, 7s. 6d.

Thausing (Prof.) Preparation of Malt and the Fabrication of Beer. 8vo, 45s.

Thomas à Kempis. See " Birthday Book."

Thompson (Emma) Wit and Wisdom of Don Quixote. Fcap. 8vo, 3s. 6d.

Thoreau. By SANBORN. (American Men of Letters.) Crown 8vo, 2s. 6d.

Through America ; or, Nine Months in the United States. By W. G. MARSHALL, M.A. With nearly 100 Woodcuts of Views of Utah country and the famous Yosemite Valley ; The Giant Trees, New York, Niagara, San Francisco, &c.; containing a full account of Mormon Life, as noted by the Author during his visits to Salt Lake City in 1878 and 1879. Demy 8vo, 21s. ; cheap edition, crown 8vo, 7s. 6d.

Through the Dark Continent: The Sources of the Nile ; Around the Great Lakes, and down the Congo. By H. M. STANLEY. Cheap Edition, crown 8vo, with some of the Illustrations and Maps, 12s. 6d.

Through Siberia. By the Rev. HENRY LANSDELL. Illustrated with about 30 Engravings, 2 Route Maps, and Photograph of the Author, in Fish-skin Costume of the Gilyaks on the Lower Amur. 2 vols., demy 8vo, 30*s.* Cheaper Edition, 1 vol., 15*s.*

Tour of the Prince of Wales in India. *See* RUSSELL.

Trees and Ferns. By F. G. HEATH. . Crown 8vo, cloth, gilt edges, with numerous Illustrations, 3*s.* 6*d.*

"A charming little volume."—*Land and Water.*

Tristram (Rev. Canon) Pathways of Palestine : A Descriptive Tour through the Holy Land. First Series. Illustrated by 44 Permanent Photographs. 2 vols., folio, cloth extra, gilt edges, 31*s.* 6*d.* each.

Turner (Edward) Studies in Russian Literature. (The Author is English Tutor in the University of St. Petersburgh.) Crown 8vo, 8*s.* 6*d.*

Two Supercargoes (The) ; or, Adventures in Savage Africa. By W. H. G. KINGSTON. Numerous Full-page Illustrations. Square imperial 16mo, cloth extra, gilt edges, 7*s.* 6*d.* ; plainer binding, 5*s.*

UNDER the Punkah. By PHIL ROBINSON, Author of "In my Indian Garden." Crown 8vo, limp cloth, 5*s.*

Union Jack (The). Every Boy's Paper. Edited by G. A. HENTY and BERNARD HELDMANN. One Penny Weekly, Monthly 6*d.* Vol. I., New Series.

The Opening Numbers will contain :—

SERIAL STORIES.

Straight : Jack Archer's Way in the World. By G. A. HENTY.
Spiggott's School Days : A Tale of Dr. Merriman's. By CUTHBERT BEDE.
Sweet Flower ; or, Red Skins and Pale Faces. By PERCY B. ST. JOHN.
Under the Meteor Flag. By HARRY COLLINGWOOD.
The White Tiger. By LOUIS BOUSSENARD. Illustrated.
A Couple of Scamps. By BERNARD HELDMANN.
Also a Serial Story by R. MOUNTNEY JEPHSON.

—— Vols. II. and III., 4to, 7*s.* 6*d.* ; gilt edges, 8*s.*

VINCENT (F.) Norsk, Lapp, and Finn. By FRANK VINCENT, Jun., Author of " The Land of the White Elephant," "Through and Through the Tropics," &c. 8vo, cloth, with Frontispiece and Map, 12*s.*

Vivian (A. P.) Wanderings in the Western Land. 3rd Edition, 10*s.* 6*d.*

BOOKS BY JULES VERNE.

CELEBRATED TRAVELS and TRAVELLERS. 3 Vols., Demy 8vo, 600 pp., upwards of 100 full-page Illustrations, 12s. 6d.; gilt edges, 14s. each :—

I. The Exploration of the World.
II. The Great Navigators of the Eighteenth Century.
III. The Great Explorers of the Nineteenth Century.

☞ The letters appended to each book refer to the various Editions and Prices given at the foot of the page.

a e TWENTY THOUSAND LEAGUES UNDER THE SEA.
a e HECTOR SERVADAC.
a e THE FUR COUNTRY.
a f FROM THE EARTH TO THE MOON, AND A TRIP ROUND IT.
a e MICHAEL STROGOFF, THE COURIER OF THE CZAR.
a e DICK SANDS, THE BOY CAPTAIN.
b c d FIVE WEEKS IN A BALLOON.
b c d ADVENTURES OF THREE ENGLISHMEN AND THREE RUSSIANS.
b c d AROUND THE WORLD IN EIGHTY DAYS.
b c { *d* A FLOATING CITY.
     { *d* THE BLOCKADE RUNNERS.
b c { *d* { DR. OX'S EXPERIMENT.
     {   { MASTER ZACHARIUS.
     { *d* { A DRAMA IN THE AIR.
     {   { A WINTER AMID THE ICE.
b c { *d* THE SURVIVORS OF THE "CHANCELLOR."
     { *d* MARTIN PAZ.
b c d THE CHILD OF THE CAVERN.
     THE MYSTERIOUS ISLAND, 3 Vols. :—
b c d I. DROPPED FROM THE CLOUDS.
b c d II. ABANDONED.
b c d III. SECRET OF THE ISLAND.
b c { *d* THE BEGUM'S FORTUNE.
     { THE MUTINEERS OF THE "BOUNTY."
b c d THE TRIBULATIONS OF A CHINAMAN.
     THE STEAM HOUSE, 2 Vols. :—
b c I. DEMON OF CAWNPORE.
b c II. TIGERS AND TRAITORS.
     THE GIANT RAFT, 2 Vols. :—
b I. EIGHT HUNDRED LEAGUES ON THE AMAZON.
b II. THE CRYPTOGRAM.
b GODFREY MORGAN.
     THE GREEN RAY. Cloth, gilt edges, 6s.

a Small 8vo, very numerous Illustrations, handsomely bound in cloth, with gilt edges, 10s. 6d.; ditto, plainer binding, 5s.
b Large imperial 16mo, very numerous Illustrations, handsomely bound in cloth, with gilt edges, 7s. 6d.
c Ditto, plainer binding, 3s. 6d.
d Cheaper Edition, 1 Vol., paper boards, with some of the Illustrations, 1s.; bound in cloth, gilt edges, 2s.
e Cheaper Edition as (*d*), in 2 Vols., 1s. each; bound in cloth, gilt edges, 1 Vol., 3s. 6d.
f Same as (*e*), except in cloth, 2 Vols., gilt edges, 2s. each.

WAITARUNA: A Story of New Zealand Life. By ALEXANDER BATHGATE, Author of "Colonial Experiences." Crown 8vo, cloth, 5s.

Waller (Rev. C. H.) The Names on the Gates of Pearl, and other Studies. By the Rev. C. H. WALLER, M.A. New Edition. Crown 8vo, cloth extra, 3s. 6d.

—— *A Grammar and Analytical Vocabulary of the Words in* the Greek Testament. Compiled from Brüder's Concordance. For the use of Divinity Students and Greek Testament Classes. By the Rev. C. H. WALLER, M.A. Part I. The Grammar. Small post 8vo, cloth, 2s. 6d. Part II. The Vocabulary, 2s. 6d.

—— *Adoption and the Covenant.* Some Thoughts on Confirmation. Super-royal 16mo, cloth limp, 2s. 6d.

—— *See also* "Silver Sockets."

Wanderings South by East: a Descriptive Record of Four Years of Travel in the less known Countries and Islands of the Southern and Eastern Hemispheres. By WALTER COOTE. 8vo, with very numerous Illustrations and a Map, 21s.

Warner (C. D.) Back-log Studies. Boards, 1s. 6d.; cloth, 2s.

—— *Mummies and Moslems.* 8vo, cloth, 12s.

Washington Irving's Little Britain. Square crown 8vo, 6s.

Weaving. See "History and Principles."

Webster. (American Men of Letters.) 18mo, 2s. 6d.

Weismann (A.) Studies in the Theory of Descent. 2 vols., 8vo, 40s.

Where to Find Ferns. By F. G. HEATH, Author of "The Fern World," &c.; with a Special Chapter on the Ferns round London; Lists of Fern Stations, and Descriptions of Ferns and Fern Habitats throughout the British Isles. Crown 8vo, cloth, price 3s.

White (Rhoda E.) From Infancy to Womanhood. A Book of Instruction for Young Mothers. Crown 8vo, cloth, 10s. 6d.

White (R. G.) England Without and Within. New Edition, crown 8vo, 10s. 6d.

Whittier (J. G.) The King's Missive, and later Poems. 18mo, choice parchment cover, 3s. 6d. This book contains all the Poems written by Mr. Whittier since the publication of "Hazel Blossoms."

—— *The Whittier Birthday Book.* Extracts from the Author's writings, with Portrait and numerous Illustrations. Uniform with the "Emerson Birthday Book." Square 16mo, very choice binding, 3s. 6d.

Wild Flowers of Switzerland. 17 Coloured Plates. 4to.
[*In preparation.*

Williams (H. W.) Diseases of the Eye. 8vo, 21s.

Wills, A Few Hints on Proving, without Professional Assistance. By a PROBATE COURT OFFICIAL. 5th Edition, revised with Forms of Wills, Residuary Accounts, &c. Fcap. 8vo, cloth limp, 1s.

Winks (W. E.) Lives of Illustrious Shoemakers. With eight Portraits. Crown 8vo, 7s. 6d.

With Axe and Rifle on the Western Prairies. By W. H. G. KINGSTON. With numerous Illustrations, square crown 8vo, cloth extra, gilt edges, 7s. 6d. ; plainer binding, 5s.

Woolsey (C. D., LL.D.) Introduction to the Study of International Law; designed as an Aid in Teaching and in Historical Studies. 5th Edition, demy 8vo, 18s.

Wreck of the Grosvenor. By W. CLARK RUSSELL, Author of " John Holdsworth, Chief Mate," " A Sailor's Sweetheart," &c. 6s. Third and Cheaper Edition.

Wright (the late Rev. Henry) The Friendship of God. With Biographical Preface by the Rev. E. H. BICKERSTETH, Portrait, &c. Crown 8vo, 6s.

YRIARTE (Charles) Florence: its History. Translated by C. B. PITMAN. Illustrated with 500 Engravings. Large imperial 4to, extra binding, gilt edges, 63s.

History ; the Medici ; the Humanists ; letters ; arts ; the Renaissance ; Illustrious Florentines ; Etruscan art ; monuments ; sculpture ; painting.

London:

SAMPSON LOW, MARSTON, SEARLE, & RIVINGTON,

CROWN BUILDINGS, 188, FLEET STREET, E.C.

www.ingramcontent.com/pod-product-compliance
Lightning Source LLC
Chambersburg PA
CBHW030405270326
41926CB00009B/1278